MULTITASKING IN GOD'S FAVOR

The Science Behind Real, Lasting Change

By

ASHTON VINES

World rights reserved. This book or any portion thereof may not be copied or reproduced in any form or manner whatever, except as provided by law, without the written permission of the publisher, except by a reviewer who may quote brief passages in a review.

The author assumes full responsibility for the accuracy of all facts and quotations as cited in this book. The opinions expressed in this book are the author's personal views and interpretations, and do not necessarily reflect those of the publisher.

This book is provided with the understanding that the publisher is not engaged in giving spiritual, legal, medical, or other professional advice. If authoritative advice is needed, the reader should seek the counsel of a competent professional.

Copyright © 2023 Ashton Vines
Copyright © 2023 TEACH Services, Inc.
ISBN-13: 978-1-4796-1510-0 (Paperback)
ISBN-13: 978-1-4796-1511-7 (ePub)
Library of Congress Control No: 2022918747

All Scripture quotations, unless otherwise indicated, are taken from the King James Version. Public domain.

All Scripture quotations marked NKJV are taken from the New King James Version®. Copyright © 1990 by Thomas Nelson. Used by permission. All rights reserved.

Published by

TEACH Services, Inc.
PUBLISHING
www.TEACHServices.com • (800) 367-1844

Table of Contents

Introduction	7
Chapter 1	11
Preparing the Vessel Step 1: Understanding	
Chapter 2	21
Preparing the Vessel Step 2: Understanding Your Weapon	
Chapter 3	35
God's Action Plan for Complete Health	
Chapter 4	59
The Antediluvian World	
Chapter 5	69
Creating Habit	
Chapter 6	83
The Process	
Chapter 7	93
The Process Continued	
Bibliography	111

Dedication

This book is dedicated to my family whose infinite love and support has always encouraged me to go on every adventure.

Also to
    Antonio T. Harris
    Man of God, Pastor, Scholar, Father, Friend

Introduction

We live in a world now that moves at an extremely high pace. Just to feel as though we are keeping up with the times, we are seemingly forced to accelerate to this rapid form of task dropping. So many things to do and so many different ways to get them done. How much more can we get done in an hour, a day, a week?

We use multitasking as this profound solution to this newfound way of life. Eliminating several of these items all at once is the goal. Just to drop these tasks from our list only to move on to the next handful and keep on grinding. We delegate and even sometimes negotiate these tasks to others just so we can concentrate on our envisaged meaningful tasks only to find that we are even further behind or overwhelmed than when we started. The list never stops growing!

With this new addiction to multitasking between devices, our focus is now being tossed back and forth like a canoe in the middle of the Atlantic Ocean during hurricane season. Media multitasking has become, and is becoming, more and more prevalent in our lives every day. As such increasing concerns for our cognitive and social/emotional well-being is rising as well, is there an issue with multitasking and does it really work? I don't know! Are we really performing at high levels as God intended for us? Or are we spinning in circles, completing a bunch of meaningless tasks that keep bringing us back to square one? We do research for projects while texting friends, checking all social media sites, shopping online, all while watching funny prank and animal videos on the tube. Our attention is being pulled in so many different directions. How can we possibly be accomplishing anything of true value?

The thing is, multitasking is generally pretty bad for our productivity, as our attention gets divided over multiple things and we end up doing none of them particularly well. This much is pretty well established, and yet wrenching ourselves free of the various distractions we face at work can be incredibly difficult.

This is perhaps because not only is multitasking something we enjoy, but we also believe it's an effective way of getting a lot of things done. That's the finding of a recent study from the University of Michigan, which explored whether this illusion of multitasking being beneficial could actually be turned into a positive.

The researchers set out to test whether shifting our perception of a task could influence how we perform at it. For instance, in one study they asked volunteers to watch a nature video, before splitting them into two groups. The first of these was the multitasking group, and they were asked to work on a learning task related to the video they'd just watched, and a transcribing task asking them to annotate the voiceover used in the video. The second group performed exactly the same tasks, but they were framed as single activities performed sequentially. All of the volunteers was then presented with a surprise quiz at the end of the tasks to test their knowledge of the video.

What did the results reveal? Well, those in the multitasking group actually performed better than their peers in the sequential group, both in terms of the number of words they transcribed and in the quality of those transcriptions. They even did better on the quiz at the end.

"The most fundamental finding is that when you take the exact same activity between these two groups you find that those who believe they are multitasking are more engaged and perform better than those who believe they're doing a single task," the authors explain.

The researchers attempted to test this finding over a further 32 experiments, with some using eye-tracking technology to monitor for user engagement with the task. When the results from all of these experiments were analyzed, the findings were consistent - when we believe we're multitasking, we are more focused on the task and perform better on it.

"Over and over and over again, across many different designs, the effect showed up, which allows us to be fairly confident that what we claim to be happening is in fact happening," they explain.

Of course we should not confuse this finding with a belief that multitasking is good for us, as previous research highlighted the neurological changes wrought by tackling many things at once. The researchers found that when we're multitasking across multiple devices at the same time, it results in lower gray-matter density in the part of our brain that is traditionally associated with both cognitive and emotional control.

"Media multitasking is becoming more prevalent in our lives today and there is increasing concern about its impacts on our cognition and social-emotional well-being. Our study was the first to reveal links between media multitasking and brain structure," the researchers say.

The researchers scanned the brains of participants whilst also asking them to complete a questionnaire detailing their use of various media. The regular use of multitasking was linked with lower brain density in the anterior cingulate cortex.

What the original research found however that such is the positive perception of multitasking, if we can trick ourselves into believing we're multitasking, we can produce higher performance levels. In the experiment both the tasks the volunteers were performing were closely aligned, which cannot be said about doing work and watching funny dog videos. The trick seems to be having tasks that are consistent in the cognitive demands they place on us.

"How close or far the nature of one task is from another could have a big effect on the outcome," the authors conclude. "In all of our experiments, they were reasonably close, but it's critical to understand how the components of each task moderate the effects that we found" (Forbes, https://1ref.us/1vc [accessed March 24, 2022]).

This is what we are all facing in 2020 and beyond. The battle is for our minds. Whatever dominates our thoughts and our focus will ultimately control our actions. All devices that can be used to distract and drive us further and further from the source of our true power will be used. Our only safeguard is to align ourselves with what God's purpose for our life truly is.

"One day of God's favor is better than a thousand days of labor."

Multitasking in God's favor puts us under the favor of God. All the areas where your mortality falls short, God fills in the gaps and continues to excel you forward day after day. The problem is we try to do it all by ourselves or by relying on man only to help us. It seems easier!

Remember the results of the multitasking experiment, though? The results shifted in favor of the ones who simply believed that they were multitasking. Therefore, they were more focused and engaged and performance was higher. The amazing power of true belief! God has already provided for all the favor we will ever need. We just need to strengthen our belief that we can have it. Just like Jesus had to grow in favor, so do we. This doesn't happen automatically or overnight. But if we train ourselves in these principles of favor and put them into practice, our lives will be forever transformed. We will grow not only in favor with God but with man as well, just as Jesus did. With Jesus at the center of everything we do, it links it all together, therefore creating a constant that renders your multitasking a successful platform. Multitasking in God's favor is the missing link to a purpose-filled life.

Chapter 1

Preparing the Vessel Step 1: Understanding

Life can be hard and in every aspect a mystery, but with the proper perspective, it can be a lot easier to live. This perspective is often deemed uneasy to achieve for some reason or another. It, too, can also be veiled from us even while sitting in plain sight. But when taken back to the root of it all, the haze begins to clear. The first step, though, in achieving this much needed perspective, of course, is in answering the age-old questions: Who are we? Why are we here? And what is our true purpose in this life? For in these three questions lies the key to everything.

If, for some reason, you wanted to put a mask over everything that was created by—and that remained precious to—your enemy, so that everyone that your enemy loved would be oblivious to its existence, what areas would you attack to conceal its truth?

What is this thing we call life? I mean, really, what is it? If you want a dictionary definition of life, it states that life is "the condition that distinguishes animals and plants from inorganic matter, including the capacity for growth, reproduction, functional activity, and continual change preceding death" (Google, https://1ref.us/1vd [accessed March 25, 2022]). OK, well what does that have to do with my much needed explanation of what this thing called life really is? Ever since the dawn of time, men and women have taken this beautiful journey and have spent a lifetime without ever understanding the vital role that they were to play in the grand design of it all. For us to attempt this, to better understand our roles, let's paint a picture real quick so that we may understand Creation and, hence, better understand the design. Of course, the best place to start for this undertaking would be the Bible, and in the beginning, of course, would be the book of Genesis.

"In the beginning God created the heaven and the earth" (Gen. 1:1).

So right here we have an all-powerful supernatural force creating what we all now recognize as home. Then he goes further: "And God said, Let there be light: and there was light" (Gen. 1:3). Now we must pay close attention to all the details in this text. Let's start with "And God said." Now these three words with a special emphasis on one ("said") goes to show that there is much power behind something just as simple as sound and God meant for it to be this way. Keep this in mind, for it shall be further revealed later in this chapter. For six days straight, God continued to create everything in this earth, and He spoke it all into existence. By the sixth day, everything seemed to be in order except one thing:

> And God said, Let us make man in our image, after our likeness: and let them have dominion over the fish of the sea, and over the fowl of the air, and over the cattle, and over all the earth, and over every creeping thing that creepeth upon the earth. So, God created man in his own image, in the image of God created he him; male and female created he them. (Gen. 1:26–27)

Everyone who has ever doubted the validity of their existence, pay close attention to these two texts, for this is the answer to the first question: Who are we? First, let's define the word image clearly: "a physical likeness or representation of a person, animal, or thing, photographed, painted, sculptured, or otherwise made visible" (Dictionary.com, https://1ref.us/1ve [accessed March 25, 2022]). Another defines it as "an optical counterpart or appearance of an object, as is produced be reflection from a mirror, refraction by a lens, or the passage of luminous rays through a small aperture and their reception on a surface" or "a mental representation; idea; conception" (Ibid. [accessed March 25, 2022]). The word likeness: which means "the fact or quality of being alike; resemblance" (Google,

"Likeness" [accessed March 25, 2022]). Are you getting the picture yet? We were created by God as a mirror image of Himself or we were a brilliant idea or concept of a higher power (God) who is of infinite intelligence or both. Either way, this concludes that we are all perfect by design. Each and every one of us is of utmost importance, and in God's plan, we are all special and essential to it being carried out. Everything that God created during the six days of Creation was spoken into existence except for one. God could have spoken us human beings into existence, but instead, He intimately formed man from the dust of the ground and breathed into his nostrils the breath of life. This was done purposely to show the importance of this creation and to represent and demonstrate God's love and attachment to mankind. This is very important for us to remember, for it sums up and better instills the reality of why God gives us so many chances to see His plan. God's desire is for us to ultimately succeed in all that we do in His name. Our problem, so often enough, is that we tend to do everything in our own name, consistently overlooking our helping Hand that can and is always ready to do wonders in our lives if, and only if, we just reach out to Him and give Him our burdens and do that which we were designed to do. Who we are and what being made in God's image means for us can be better understood by exploring the beginning of time, yes, but it can be even better understood by studying the people therein.

So, come with me for a moment back in time to a young world. A world that was fresh and vibrant and full of wonder. Where it all started in the Garden of Eden, where Adam and Eve dwelt and had dominion over all the earth. After so many years peacefully in the garden, though, the Bible isn't specific about the actual length of time. Anyway, we know that Eve was tempted by a serpent and when Adam partakes of the fruit with her from the tree of knowledge of good and evil, they both became aware of sin and God was displeased. At that moment, they realized they were naked and were both banished from Eden and life became hard for them in every way as a result of sin. But prior to this, we are led to believe that Adam personally communicated with God on a regular basis. In Genesis 2:15–17 it says, "And the LORD God took the man, and put him into the garden of Eden to dress it and to keep it. And the LORD God commanded the man, saying, Of every tree of the garden thou mayest freely eat: But of the tree of the knowledge of good and evil, thou shalt not eat of it" (emphasis mine). This is the first implementation of God's plan—the first test. Do we do it God's way or our way? Also, when we look at verse 19, we see that God brought every beast of the field and fowl of the air to Adam to see what he would call them. Really look at this for a moment because here we see a relationship forming between God and Adam. In this we must assume that God was personally teaching Adam everything about this material and spiritual world, especially if He was assigning him the task of dressing it and keeping it. Again, we see God equipping us with everything we need to be successful. He wants you to succeed! If Adam was able to commune with God face-to-face and was able to receive endless knowledge straight from the Creator, Adam had to be a marvelous creature. The mere fact that he was able to be in God's presence alone without dying shows that Adam possessed great power given to him by God. As a result of sin, Adam lost face-to-face communion with God and his task had to change. He was now commanded to instruct his posterity or offspring in the way of the Lord (White, *Education*, pp. 14–15). Adam treasured what God had unveiled to him, and he faithfully passed it on to his succeeding generations. This was the beginning of the gospel. "Gospel" means a thing that is absolutely true. God's instructions were made clear to Adam and of absolute truth, so he obeyed. No longer in the garden, without access to the tree of life, death was an inescapable reality at this point, and the time that was spent on this earth now became a purpose-driven destiny for all. Adam lived a life that was full of sorrow—a lot of humility and contrition he would have to witness. He had to endure the death of his own son, Abel, that was killed by his other son, Cain. The mere horror of this alone must have brought Adam to his knees. How could such corruption be possible by his own flesh and blood? The presence of sin made life hard to live then. Outside of the garden, man was now departed from God's initial grand design for what life was to be. Man was now separated from the Father and was no longer fit to be in His presence. What Adam was now instructed to do was to teach his children the new way of coming to the Father that was to be based entirely upon faith and obedience. Cain and Abel were the first generation born into sin. Imagine what it was like for them growing up hearing all the grand stories of the Garden of Eden. Hearing of all the beautiful animals and vegetation that stretched for miles—that Adam was able to name and be master of. Of all this splendor, to now be looking upon a sin-cursed ground that with every toil, resonated punishment for sins they hadn't even committed, Cain and Abel grew up now sacrificing a lamb as offering to God. It was now through the blood shed of the spotless lamb that man was to be reminded that the only way back to the Father was through the Redeemer. The blood signified the blood that Jesus would shed for our sins because only by the shedding of blood is there any true atonement for our sins (Heb. 9:22). Cain and Abel understood these offerings very well and the purpose for them and, through faith, obediently performed them with their parents. These offerings required total faith, obedience, and submission to God.

Faith—That one day God would send His Son to be sacrificed for our sins so that we may be redeemed and once again have a way to the Father.

Obedience—Total attention to detail of every aspect of the offering, distinctly articulated by God to represent future things to come.

Submission—By being obedient, this allowed God to fulfill His purpose through them for spreading hope to all.

This, my friends, is the answer to the second question: "Why are we here?" Our job is to have total and complete faith and submission to God, for it is only then that we give Him permission to use us to spread hope to His children. Abel understood this concept very well and lived it through his offering, which was perfectly done each time because he followed perfectly orchestrated instructions every time. Now this is the part when we begin to see the human condition rear its ugly head with Cain. I'm sure with all the stories he had to hear and the fact that he could actually still see the

Garden of Eden—evidence that all the stories were true—must have taken a toll on him in a negative way because he allowed it to. He began to resent God for the punishment handed out to his parents that he now had to endure as well. He began to allow Satan to cloud his thoughts with selfish ones, thoughts of rebellion toward the Creator because "nothing could be as good as the Garden of Eden" and "nothing could be deserving of this punishment." We all know how that turned out. Abel's offering was accepted and a sign from heaven was sent down to acknowledge his offering. Cain's offering was denied, and no sign was given because he disobeyed simple instruction and brought the first fruits of the ground of which he tilled. He offered no shedding of blood; his actions signified defiance, not submission. Then Cain, still being led by delusions from Satan, ended the life of his own brother (Gen. 4:1–18) because of his warped perception of nepotism. This is how Satan works; he has people so self-indulged that they don't even see their wrongdoing anymore and don't find themselves deserving of any reproof or punishment for that matter. He clouds their judgements over time so much so that, with one decision after another, they find themselves deeper and deeper in sin—the very process that proved to be an ongoing human condition and that would last for thousands and thousands of years.

And so, it began the journey of the greatest generation to ever walk this earth. The generation that God had blessed with incomparable power that this earth would never have the pleasure of witnessing again, with these rare abilities to plan and execute on a scale that men of today could only dream of. The generation that had in their midst, for hundreds of years, the human that was created in God's very own image, the man that was instructed by God Himself in all wisdom of this world—yes, the antediluvians were a blessed people. Basking in all knowledge and wisdom of this world, to be able to visually see God's wonderful hand in the breathtakingly landscaped view of Eden still in their presence. Superior strength and stature and a cunning eye for detail—no! There's no way this generation could turn their back on God.

The word "antediluvian" means "of or belonging to the time before the biblical Flood" (Google, "Antediluvian," https://1ref.us/1vf [accessed March 25, 2022]). Some of the greatest names that are etched in earth's history came from this era: Adam, Abel, Seth, Enoch, Methuselah, and Noah. When most people think of the beginning of time, thanks to the far-stretched ideology of evolution, they tend to see our humble beginning as a bunch of cavemen that had to learn everything about this earth on their own. This tends to paint a picture of a primitive creature not so far removed from the beasts that crawl and inhabit this world alongside us. Such a thought is in such opposition with the Bible, for in Genesis 1:28 it reads:

> And God blessed them, and God said unto them, Be fruitful, and multiply, and replenish the earth, and subdue it: and have dominion over the fish of the sea, and over the fowl of the air, and over every living thing that moveth upon the earth.

The two keywords from this text to put into context the capabilities of that generation are "subdue" (to bring under control) and "dominion" (sovereignty; control). We see nowadays how hard it can be to go up against mother nature and how quickly we can be reminded of how feeble we really are at times. This was not always the case, nor the vision, God had for us as a people. For to conquer earth in all of its vast and wondrous enigmatic elements, that enabled human body had to be able to reciprocate such qualities in greater proportion. That's why we were blessed with a functioning brain, with the ability of social intelligence, planning, and reasoning. So, people coming from tadpoles, monkeys, or whatever and evolving into cavemen who knew nothing was simply not the case. These men and women were taught by Adam who was personally taught by the CREATOR. Such a premise leaves no room for ignorance.

The antediluvian people were a powerful people that walked the earth for extended periods of time. Their time was measured in centuries. Methuselah alone lived 969 years; imagine what could be accomplished if given that much time on this earth. You see, those who followed God in those days had a job to do, and that was the will of God. God endowed them with all the power and time they would need in order to accomplish this.

"Had that long-lived people, with their rare powers to plan and execute, devoted themselves to the service of God, they would have made their Creator's name a praise in the earth, and would have answered the purpose for which He gave them life" (White, *Patriarchs and Prophets*, p. 90).

In Genesis 6:4 it states that "[t]here were giants in the earth in those days," mighty men which were of old, men of renown. The antediluvians were taller than we are now, stronger than we are now, and much smarter than we all are now. If we only, supposedly, use about 10 percent of our brain mass consciously nowadays, hence the need for computers—which, in fact, were modeled after the human brain. Picture God allowing them to consciously use a considerably larger percentage of their brain mass and vividly imagine the possibilities of that era. Amazing artifacts created in ways still unexplainable today and amassed as giant terms of endearment. Inventions that defy today's logic and were based off of knowledge gained firsthand by the Creator's first pupil (Adam). The antediluvians used to study animals and their natural habitat and were able to comprehend the results instantaneously and convert it to fit whatever application that was imagined. Imagine now for a second that the Wright brothers weren't the first to master flight and that the first flying machines could have probably been much more sophisticated and in harmony with natures' law—as in to preserve it, not pollute it. Haven't you ever heard the term "there is nothing new under the sun" (Eccles. 1:9)? The antediluvians needed no books, no computers, no tablets, no cameras, and no fancy watches that talk. With their huge mental capacities, they had very strong memories and could pull from them consciously whenever they wanted. These are the people that we are descendants of; we are a powerful people. Though much has been decreased, we still have many capabilities, and the possibilities are endless. The sooner we understand who we are and who we really represent, the sooner we become ready to carry a message for our Creator. God blessed these men and women with these great gifts in order to carry out His plan. "With great power comes great responsibility." Instead, many of them, unfortunately, shut God out and became consumed with self-adornment, corrupt passions, and any and all pleasures that were imagined continually. They took up many other gods before the true Creator. Now you would think that with all this power, long life, and ability—as well as a true knowledge of how and why they existed—that they would have been more resistant to sin and eager to please their Creator. But it was the complete opposite for most of humankind, and because they were so great and powerful, they sinned to the extent of their abilities and just continued to get worse and worse.

But there is still a message to be carried out. There has always been a message to spread to all of them that love God and want to get to know Him. God also still gives those who are deserving this same power that was granted to the antediluvians and equips them with everything that they need to fulfill His work. This brings us now to the answer to the final question: What is our true purpose? Our purpose ever since the exiting of Eden has always been to carry out the work of our Creator. If you look at the lineage of Adam and the meanings of their names, all the way to Noah—the line that represented the true followers of God in a corrupt world—the answer and message is made very clear:

Adam = Man of the earth

Seth = Appointed

Enosh = Mortal

Cainan = Sorrow

Mahalalel = The Blessed God

Jared = Shall come down / he who descended

Enoch = Teaching

Methuselah = His death shall bring

Lamech = The Despairing

Noah = Comfort

"Man of the earth appointed mortal sorrow, the blessed God shall come down teaching and his death shall bring the despairing comfort." (This is according to my research of the meaning of these different names.)

The message of their time was to tell of a Savior that would come down and take our place. To tell of a Savior that cares for us and loves us so much that He would die to cover our sins. This was the gospel leading up to Jesus dying on the cross. Now, present day, our mission is to spread the same hope to all, of the second coming of the Savior that will come this time to take all who love Him and keep His commandments home to be with Him for all eternity. See, the purpose has and always will be to do God's will, spread His love, and to take His gospel in whatever form it may be (along as it's in accordance with the Bible and God's will) unto all the world.

Chapter 2

Preparing the Vessel Step 2: Understanding Your Weapon

The effects of eating habits on the mind —the basis of all human productivity—is astounding. Our eating habits, good or bad, affect our daily production by manipulating mind, body, and spirit. The right foods can produce productive benefits in vast proportions. The wrong foods become catalysts of contrary affects. In other words, we become what we eat.

We are the captains of our vessels. Picture for a moment an aircraft carrier floating peacefully in the harbor. Now, before this ship is even considered battle ready, it must undergo a series of quality checks to ensure that, if given a mission, it has what it needs to be able to complete this mission successfully. Since the engine is the core of the ship, let's start there. I'm pretty sure it is checked for proper lubricant levels, fuel, hydraulic pressures, water, all nuclear power sources, and backup power sources. Also, since the massive computer system onboard is the brain of the ship, of which without it the ship does not work in harmony at all, this entire system is checked to ensure that all circuitry is in the proper order, especially since those pathways link the entire ship together. It even links the system to its power source, for without that key component, its function wouldn't exist. The ship is carefully monitored for any and all issues that could potentially derail any forms of forward progress once launched and is logged immediately so that repairs may be made beforehand. An aircraft carrier is given the best of everything so that it is always ready for whatever it may encounter on its journey. Now, to the question that all of mankind faces: If we are all commissioned by God to complete His mission, are we preparing for Him a proper warship that can withstand any storm?

As the mind works as an ultimate computer, it transmits working commands throughout the body. One can either defer or heighten daily intellectual conception and production ability by what is placed in the body for nourishment. However, to really grasp this, first it must be understood how the mind works as a result to conception. To do this, a few areas of the brain need to be explored. Especially one that is considered the center of traffic in the superhighways of the human mind. What is conception? Conception is ... well, there are three very good definitions—the forming or devising of a plan or idea, the way in which something is perceived or regarded, or a general notion; an abstract idea (Google, "Conception," https://1ref.us/1vg [accessed March 28, 2022]). Now, to understand conception and the importance of its relative effectiveness to the human mind for the ability to recognize and accept an assignment from God is huge. In order to progress to this level of awareness, one must understand where each job is designated in the mind. The areas in which we will explore will take us through the frontal lobes, the inhibitory mechanisms of the cortex, the limbic system, and, finally, the reticular activating system.

The Frontal Lobes

The frontal lobes play a vital role in who we are as individuals. The pieces that make each one of us uniquely different all start here in the frontal lobes. The frontal lobes, in essence, are the control panel of the human personality. It gives us our ability to communicate and is responsible for our primary motor functions, thus, giving us our ability to consciously move our muscles and our two key areas related to speech. We use our frontal lobes every day. We use it to make simple decisions such as what to eat for breakfast in the morning or for more complex tasks such as planning our week or studying for an exam. The frontal lobes are responsible for the ability to pay attention and focus our concentration. It also helps us learn and remember what we have learned and behave appropriately for every situation by controlling emotional expression and sexual behaviors. Of all the creatures God created, our frontal lobes are larger and more developed than any other organism (Lumen, "Structure and Function of the Brain," https://1ref.us/1wn [accessed May 10, 2022]).

The Inhibitory Mechanisms of the Cortex

The inhibitory mechanisms of the cortex regulate our actions and keeps us from hyperactivity. It keeps us from getting mad at the wrong times and from saying things out of turn as well. About 70 percent of our brain exists primarily to keep the other 30 percent in check. Without these inhibitory mechanisms, humans would have no self-control. Sometimes these areas of the brain don't work as hard as they ought to. This results in what is often called disinhibition disorders. When we see such impulsive behaviors, quick tempers, poor decision making, and hyperactivity, this is often the root cause of such actions (Lumen, "Structure and Function of the Brain," https://1ref.us/1wn [accessed May 10, 2022]).

The Limbic System

The limbic system plays a vital role in our day-to-day lives. Our days are merely a series of choices that are compounded upon one another to create productivity or the lack of productivity. We as humans often base our decisions off sheer mood. The way we feel at the precise moment a multi-optional buffet presents itself and we are forced to choose. This is why we must take time to understand what drives this conscious and unconscious action that is carried out numerous times throughout our entire day, every day of our lives. The average person makes about 35,000 conscious decisions a day. Now there is no way to accurately measure the true amount per day. So, simply for the sake of envisioning how our lives are shaped on a day-to-day basis by our decisions, we must understand that the limbic system is the base of emotion. So essentially it is the major driver of our day-to-day operations, since we make the bulk of our decisions emotionally.

    The limbic system is basically a highly attentive lookout post. It can be over-activated, causing a person to have mood swings or quick temper outbursts. If a person is over-aroused, they may also startle easily, touch everything around them, and be hypervigilant. A limbic system under normal conditions provides for normal emotional changes, normal levels of energy, regular sleep patterns, and normal levels of coping with stress. If a limbic system is dysfunctional, it results in problems in these general areas.

> The limbic system is a complex set of structures found on the central underside of the cerebrum, comprising inner sections of the temporal lobes and the bottom of the frontal lobe. It combines higher mental functions and primitive emotion into a single system often referred to as the emotional nervous system. It is not only responsible for our emotional lives but also our higher mental functions, such as learning and formation of memories. The limbic system is the reason that some physical things such as eating seem so pleasurable to us, and the reason why some medical conditions, such as high blood pressure, are caused by mental stress. (Lumen, "Structure and Function of the Brain," https://1ref.us/1wn [accessed May 10, 2022])

There are six primary structures that make up the limbic system. Let's explore each of them a little deeper as to understand their purpose and their relationship with the body as a whole. They are known as the amygdala, the hippocampus, the thalamus and hypothalamus, the cingulate gyrus, and the basal ganglia. These structures all play an indispensable role individually as well as collectively in the continued successful function of the limbic system.

The Amygdala

The amygdala, with its small oval-shaped structure, is the emotion center of the brain. We, as humans, possess two of these located in both the left and right temporal lobes. The amygdala is responsible for categorizing our emotional responses to surrounding stimuli based off emotional valence. In other words, it's the reason why the brain has the ability to recognize a potential threat and prepare the body to react accordingly. If you have ever wondered why, when you are scared, your heart rate increases and your rate of breathing gets heavy, meet the culprit: the amygdala. These emotional responses can also be triggered by our imaginations; that's why it's so important what we focus our thoughts on daily. Our reflexive brain (amygdala and nucleus accumbens) receives internal, as well as external, sensory information and reacts instinctively to protect you from any danger. This is why the amygdala is categorized as the reason for our ability to learn through reward and punishment, a key factor in creating new habits. The bigger the emotional arousal attached to an event, the stronger the memory of that event. So, since the amygdala is involved in the modulation of memory consolidation, it is important to remember that the greater the emotional arousal during a learning exercise, the greater the retention of that memory (Lumen, "Structure and Function of the Brain," https://1ref.us/1wn [accessed May 10, 2022]).

The Hippocampus

This little one lies deep in the temporal lobe and has two horns curving back from the amygdala. The hippocampus is responsible for the formation of new memories of past events. It is also known to be responsible for declarative memory, which are memories that can be verbalized, like facts and episodic memory (Lumen, "Structure and Function of the Brain," https://1ref.us/1wn [accessed May 10, 2022]). The relationship between emotion and memory is quite astounding. In fact, they are so closely related I don't think you can have one without the other. For example, imagine for a moment going to a new church and being introduced to a lot of people. Which people do you think you'd actually end up remembering by their first name? Would it be the beautiful couple that had two beautiful babies and greeted you with the two biggest smiles you have ever seen? Or would you remember the two ladies that said hi and bye, pretty much walked off quickly after stating their names? Would you remember the young man that you were introduced to right before service began not knowing that you would hear his voice sound out with amazing melodies that would end up bringing you to tears of joy right before the speaker preached? It's the emotion attached to the experience that solidifies a new memory. That is why the limbic system, which you know as the emotion center of the brain, is in charge of transferring information into new memory, and the bulk of all this transferring happens right in the hippocampus. If the hippocampus is damaged in any way, it could lead to great difficulties in forming new memories. One way in which a hippocampus can become damaged is through shrinkage; yes, the hippocampus tends to shrink as the years go by. Studies have shown that stress is one of the main causes of hippocampal shrinkage. But, praise the Lord, we can reverse the process. More on that in later chapters.

The Thalamus and Hypothalamus

The thalamus is a grape-shaped structure that rests beneath the corpus callosum. It acts as a relay station for impulses flowing to and from the brain stem, spinal cord, cerebellum, and cerebrum. Imagine the old-school switchboard operators patching every signal to its correct pathway. Same is the function of the thalamus, directing sensory input to its correct pathway in the cerebral cortex. It's actually in charge of all the sensory input coming in from all of the senses, except for one: smell. Both the thalamus and the hypothalamus are associated with changes in emotional reactivity based off input received from the senses. The hypothalamus plays an important role for many internal bodily functions. It monitors hormone concentrations, body temperature, and water concentration. Feelings of rage, hunger, aggressive behavior, and general thirst can all be attributed to the hypothalamus. If there are injured regions in the hypothalamus, they can interfere with many unconscious functions, like respiration and metabolism. It can also affect motivated behaviors as well, such as hunger, combativeness, and sexuality. The hypothalamus also acts as a go-between for the nervous system and the endocrine system (hormones). It has many connections with the pituitary gland and has the ability to produce and regulate hormones

(Lumen, "Structure and Function of the Brain," https://1ref.us/1wn [accessed May 10, 2022]).

The Cingulate Gyrus

The cingulate gyrus has five layers and sits atop the corpus callosum and can be divided into two segments. The first being the anterior cingulate, which is responsible for vocalizing and emotional motor functions involving the hands. It's also responsible for regulating autonomic and endocrine activities. The second segment, the posterior cingulate, is involved in visual-spatial and tactile analysis. This part also handles motor output and memory. The anterior cingulate processes and modulates the expression of emotional nuances, emotional learning, and vocalization. It enables the possibility of motivationally significant goal-directed behavior by forming long-term attachments and maternal behavior. On the other hand, the posterior cingulate integrates visual input with motoric output while paying no mind to emotional stimuli. It's also involved in visual-spatial and memory-cognitive activities. As it relates to body and movement, I guess you can say that this area is responsible for the ability of creating muscle memory (Lumen, "Structure and Function of the Brain," https://1ref.us/1wn [accessed May 10, 2022]).

The Basal Ganglia

The basal ganglia are a group of nuclei that live deep in the white matter of the frontal lobes. They are at the base of the forebrain and are immensely interconnected with the cerebral cortex, thalamus, and other areas of the brain. These little guys are responsible for organizing motor behavior, habit learning, predictive control, and temporal sequencing. Many theories around today suggest that the basal ganglia is in charge of action selection. When the inhibitory influence that these nuclei have over so many motor systems release their inhibition, causing these systems to become extremely active, it's very hard to deny these theories. These actions are triggered from signals that are sent from all over the brain to the basal ganglia. The prefrontal cortex is one of these areas sending signals, which plays an important role in executive functions (Lumen, "Structure and Function of the Brain," https://1ref.us/1wn [accessed May 10, 2022]).

The Reticular Activating System

Now it's time to introduce you to the reticular activating system, also considered to be the center of all major traffic in the human mind. The RAS is the attention center in the brain, and it is the key to turning on the brain. It is also a huge component in driving motivation. This wonderful, somewhat magical, structure is connected, at its base, to the spinal cord, where it receives information projected directly from the ascending sensory tracts (the five senses). Consisting of very complex neurons, the RAS serves as a point of convergence, per se, for signals from the external world to be brought to your internal environment. This is a result of the brain stem reticular formation running all the way up the midbrain. In other words, this is the part of the brain where the outside world and your thoughts and inner feelings meet (Lumen, "Structure and Function of the Brain," https://1ref.us/1wn [accessed May 10, 2022]).

The RAS is very capable of generating dynamic effects on the activity that takes place in the cerebral cortex. The cerebral is a thin, convoluted (rolled) surface layer of gray matter on the cerebral hemispheres (halves of the brain). They consist, principally, of cell bodies of neurons arranged in five layers, along with numerous fibers. The RAS also has an effect on the frontal lobes and the motor activity centers of the brain.

This system is the center of balance for the other systems involved in learning, self-control, inhibitions, and motivation. When it functions properly, it provides the neural connections that are needed for the processing and learning of information. The RAS also sequences the ability to pay attention to the correct task. If the RAS doesn't excite neurons in the cortex, it causes an under-aroused cortex. Within an under-aroused cortex, there is difficulty learning, poor memory, little self-control, and many other negative effects. As a matter of fact, if the RAS didn't activate the cortex at all, it would produce a coma like state. Now if the RAS is too excited and arouses the brain in excess, it causes an excessive startle response, hyper vigilance, touching everything, talking too much, restlessness, and very hyperactive. In order to achieve proper brain function, it is of utmost importance that the RAS be activated to normal levels (Lumen, "Structure and Function of the Brain," https://1ref.us/1wn [accessed May 10, 2022]). The reticular activating system can be your most valuable tool for productivity in every aspect of your life, if cared for properly. We will learn more on how to use this wonderful piece of ourselves that God blessed us with, in order to achieve greatness, in later chapters.

So now, you're probably asking, "How is knowing all this about the brain supposed to help me be more productive?" or "How is this supposed to help me communicate with God and allow Him to use me as a vessel to spread His love?" Well, here you go! In order for God to be able to use us efficiently, our minds need to be at optimum operating proficiency. Anything that we do for God should be done to the best of our ability, and God will take care of the rest. Now that's not to say that God can't take anyone from any background and use them effectively, because He can and He has. But if we are true followers of Christ, we should want to give Him the best of everything to work with. We should prove ourselves trustworthy continuously by being faithful stewards of the most precious gift God has given us: our bodies.

The brain, with all of its wonderful components, operates off of what you place in it. The level of effectiveness is solely up to you, by your choice of fuel. If you own a high-performing sports car, are you going to fill it with cheap gas and expect it to continue to operate at a high level? No, you're not, because that car comes with specific instructions not to use anything but high-octane gas; anything else just will not cut it. If you want to maintain the same performance you've been getting and not have your car knocking, you must operate within the guidelines. Everything in this car and its process is carefully thought out. The engineers know how the car will burn the fuel, the rate at which it will be burned, and the output of such burning in the form of acceleration. The same should be for our bodies. We should know what we are putting in our bodies and know what it will produce once in there.

Neurotransmitters

A neurotransmitter is a chemical that transmits signals or messages from one neuron to the next across synapses. In certain foods, there are nutrients that are forerunners to neurotransmitters. The amount of a forerunner nutrient in your diet determines how much of its following neurotransmitter you will produce. Simply said, the wrong food in in your body, and your mind, lacks the neural density to process incoming information. Imagine a piece of conduit and visualize the incoming information being processed as a volume of water. If the brain doesn't have enough neural density or connections, then it will be like a piece of conduit that is too small to handle a large volume of water. Some of the information will get to its destination and be processed and learned, and the rest will be lost, like the water splashing out of an overflowing pipe (Lumen, "Structure and Function of the Brain," https://1ref.us/1wn [accessed May 10, 2022]).

The best way to ensure proper intake of the right nutrients for optimum neurotransmitter function is to first know what kinds of neurotransmitters there are and how many there actually are. Since the discovery of such wonderful little workers in 1934, more than 100 of these chemical messengers have been distinctly identified. The easiest way to classify them is by dividing them into these seven categories:

> **Amino acids**: glutamate, aspartate, D-serine, y-aminobutyric acid, glycine, etc.
>
> **Gasotransmitters**: nitric oxide, carbon monoxide, hydrogen sulfide, etc.
>
> **Monoamines**: dopamine, norepinephrine, epinephrine, histamine, serotonin, etc.

Trace amines: phenethylamine, N-methylphenethylamine, 3-iodothyronamine, tyramine, octopamine, tryptamine, etc.

Peptides: substance P, somatostatin, opioid peptides, cocaine and amphetamine regulated transcript, etc.

Purines: adenosine, adenosine triphosphate, etc.

Others: acetylcholine, anandamide, etc. (Wikipedia, "Neurotransmitter," https://1ref.us/1vh [accessed March 29, 2022]).

Primarily, amino acids are the main neurotransmitters that are received through our diets. Our bodies then use these nutrients found in the foods we eat to manufacture other neurotransmitters. There are eighty amino acids found in nature, however, only twenty are necessary for human metabolism or growth. Some of these amino acids can be found in foods and the others the body can produce for itself. Also, the amino acids that must be received through diet are called essentials and are also known as histidine, which simply means essential for human tissue repair and growth. These amino acids are recognized by these names: histidine, isoleucine, leucine, lysine, methionine, phenylalanine, threonine, tryptophan, and valine (Healthline, "9 Important Functions of Protein," https://1ref.us/1vi [accessed March 29, 2022]). The other amino acids that are produced in the body are known as nonessentials.

As we have learned so far, amino acids quite commonly act as forerunners for other neurotransmitters, such as serotonin. Serotonin is a hormone found in the intestine and CNS neurons. This wonderful hormone exists in order to keep your mood upbeat. Serotonin is made from tryptophan, an amino acid found in seaweed, spinach, mustard greens, watercress, asparagus, and broccoli rabe (Wikipedia, "Neurotransmitter," https://1ref.us/1vh [accessed March 29, 2022]). You can also get tryptophan from certain meats and dairy, but everyone could use a few more veggies in their life. Vitamins such as iron, zinc, B3, B6, and C help facilitate the enzymatic reactions necessary to convert tryptophan to serotonin.

Unfortunately, there are a wide range of problems affiliated with improper levels of serotonin. Depression, anxiety, moodiness, inability to make clear decisions, and the like, are all a byproduct of serotonin deficiencies (Ibid., [accessed March 29, 2022]). This can be a major factor in zeroing in on the primary interferences of your daily productivity. So, in essence, by supplementing your diet with plenty of amino acids, you can consistently counteract low levels of serotonin.

There are other neurotransmitters that rely on the transforming power of amino acids. One being GABA, which aids the brain in filtering out extraneous information (Wikipedia, "gamma-aminobutyric acid," https://1ref.us/1wo [accessed May 10, 2022]). This internally allows your brain to stay focused and calm. Glutamine, also an amino acid, is the principal building block of GABA and can be found in legumes, halibut, brown rice, and spinach (Wikipedia, "Glutamine," https://1ref.us/1wp [accessed May 10, 2022]). There are always vitamins or minerals associated with the enzymatic reactions necessary for conversion. In this case, vitamins B3, B6, and B12 are responsible for the conversion of glutamine to GABA.

The most powerful of the stimulating neurotransmitters is dopamine. Dopamine is responsible for many of the highs that the body feels. The amino acid that is present in this conversion is tyrosine—found in protein (Wikipedia, "Neurotransmitter," https://1ref.us/1vh [accessed March 29, 2022]). The brain converts tyrosine to dopamine using folic acid, vitamin B6, magnesium, and zinc. You can find tyrosine in avocado, almonds, dairy, pumpkin seeds, and sesame seeds. Another stimulating neurotransmitter is norepinephrine, and it is made from dopamine (Wikipedia, "Norepinephrine," https://1ref.us/1wq [accessed May 10, 2022]). The brain uses dopamine with some help from the mineral copper, vitamins B6 and C to make norepinephrine (Wikipedia, "Dopamine," https://1ref.us/1wr [accessed May 10, 2022]). Norepinephrine is also derived from the amino acid tyrosine (Wikipedia, "Tyrosine," https://1ref.us/1ws [accessed May 10, 2022]).

Now that we understand how nutrients affect us on a chemical level, we must acknowledge the simple fact that our emotions drive our thoughts that, in turn, form our beliefs, which ultimately control our actions. It all starts with what we place in our vessels each and every day. If you wanted a government of your own and you wanted to be able to control your people, thinking strategically what areas would you attack first, they say that the quickest way to a man's heart is through his stomach. Did you know that the food industry in the United States is the number one leading contributor to the gross national product? This industry is HUGE and look at the by-product that we see in this country because of it. Heart disease, cancer, diabetes, growth abnormalities, and more and more allergies being discovered each year, and that's just naming a few of the health concerns this country faces. When you look at all of the food being advertised, and if you were to break down most of these item's ingredients, you would find little to no true nutritional value at all. So, for all of us on this fast-food diet, how much do you think this is affecting our emotions?

Now that you understand what happens to us on a chemical level and what the body needs, how much do you think this diet affects our thoughts? Oh, and how is your belief system right now? Is it positive or negative? Do you have the relationship that you want with God and everyone else in your life? Maybe that is a little too thought provoking, but sometimes—quite often—the look inward is needed. Your action is suffering because of the lack of personal control over your emotions, your thoughts, and your beliefs. If you are not controlling yourself, if you are not allowing God to control you, then who is?

We as humans possess the most wonderful gift besides life. We have a mind that can learn and improve upon itself through itself. Every day we are presented with choices. Choices that will determine how successful and productive each day will be. This is our true battle: living each day purposefully. It can either be aided through the conditioning of our bodies (vessels) so that we may perform at the top of our abilities or we can defer our thinking and spend all day playing catch up, emotionally torn in every direction. God has blessed us with all the resources for greatness. The ultimate blessing is the choice!

"And Joshua said unto all the people [of Israel], '… choose you this day whom ye will serve … but as for me and my house, we will serve the LORD'" (Josh. 24:2, 15).

Chapter 3

God's Action Plan for Complete Health

"Beloved, I wish above all things that thou mayest prosper and be in health, even as thy soul prospereth" (3 John 2). True religion and the laws of health go hand in hand. It is impossible to work for the salvation of men and women without presenting to them the need of breaking away from sinful gratifications which destroy the health, debase the soul, and prevent divine truth from impressing the mind. "Men and women must be taught to take a careful review of every habit and practice, and at once put away those things that cause an unhealthy condition of the body, and thus cast a dark shadow over the mind" (White, *Counsels on Health*, p. 445).

Did God ever have a plan for our health? If so, what would this plan look like? Has this plan been around for ages? Does this plan really work if correctly applied to all lives? The answer is yes! God has and will always have an action plan conducive to our good health.

God has always had an action plan for our health since Creation. "And God said, Behold, I have given you every herb bearing seed, which is upon the face of all the earth, and every tree, in the which is the fruit of a tree yielding seed; to you it shall be for meat" (Gen. 1:29). This health message has been available to all the generations, not just us in modern times but all since the beginning—and to all races in every country. For us to be able to recognize this message to be from God and for it to be able to reside within a divine outline, He designed it with some certain criteria:

1. It had to be available to all generations since Creation.
2. It could not be available only to people in the twentieth century or only in developed countries. It could not involve any high technology.

3. It would have to be able to be done at home.
4. It would have to be able to be understood by all, educated or not educated. It must be 100 percent natural.
5. It must be inexpensive so the poor could also use it. It would cause absolutely no harm to the body.
6. It would not depend on torturing and death of myriads of God's creatures to develop it. It would not require skilled personnel to administer it.
7. It would not use items so poisonous that a small error in dose is deadly. It would be available to all, not just a privileged few.

With all the modern diets and plans that exist today, there are none that meet all these requirements: This is God's action plan for our health and well-being. He has thrown it out to all of us, to give vibrancy of life. Blessed be to all that take full advantage of God's wonderful gifts.

There are eight key components that make up this life-giving plan that God has laid out for us to follow, if we so choose. Join me as we explore each one, so that we may work to remove all hindrances that keep us from living the life that God intended us to live.

"My people are destroyed for lack of knowledge: because thou hast rejected knowledge, I will also reject thee, that thou shalt be no priest to me: seeing thou has forgotten the law of thy God, I will also forget thy children" (Hosea 4:6).

Nutrition

Adam and Eve set the fate of all humanity through the indulgence of appetite. Woe be it unto us to make that same mistake. God has given us all the resources for us to sustain good health, and nowadays it's as easy to come by as a trip to our local health food or grocery store. It just requires a little education to possess the know-how necessary to turn healthy foods into an array of palatable options. Today, with the over commercialization of "diets," I think the real meaning of diet has been lost in translation for most. People now see a new trending diet on TV and figure, "If I just get that diet along with all its products in my house, the diet will take care of the rest." As if it's alive or is a functioning robot that will come in and do everything and the consumer won't have to lift a finger. No need to change any horrible, health-decreasing habits—just get the diet and put it on the shelf in the kitchen and watch it go to work.

Sorry, a diet is simply the sum of food and drink a person consumes habitually. The key word being habitually. It takes twenty-one days to create a habit and I would say twice as long to break a bad one by solidifying a replacement practice. Making significant changes in one's daily diet requires thought, planning, education, and an array of good choices throughout each day. There are ten simple guidelines for healthy eating that can be very helpful.

1. Eat a variety of fruits, nuts, grains, veggies, legumes, and seeds
2. Minimize fat, salt, and sugar intake
3. Try to avoid animal protein
4. Eat at regular times
5. Always eat a balanced breakfast, an energy-packed lunch, and light dinner
6. Avoid eating late at night
7. Avoid eating between meals—allow 3–5 hours between meals
8. Careful of your combination of foods (don't mix fruits and veggies)
9. No refined grains
10. Go for good blood building foods

Breakfast

Breakfast is so important. Yeah, I know, it sounds so cliché. Fast-forward now to modern day. Who has time for breakfast, right? There's money to be made, kids to be fed and tended to, oh and don't forget the never-ending to-do list that just seems to grow with each day. Breakfast? Hold up, the Danish counts right? Or maybe the doughnut that was had with that nice tall venti latte—that was just so amazing, might I add. All of that was a wonderful, well-balanced breakfast, right? I mean I balanced it perfectly between both of my hands. Unfortunately, this is reality for so many people today—always on the go. Too busy to take a few moments to stop and eat or to at least make plans to have something that is healthy that can be eaten on the go.

Breakfast, also known as break-fast, is essential for providing the body and brain with fuel after a long night of fasting. Hence the name! Without breakfast, the body is literally running on empty, just like the sports car mentioned earlier. If the manual says to use high octane gas for optimum performance, you're not going to use the weakest fuel at the gas station, right? Well, the body must run on fuel as well. What do you think would happen to the sports car if the owner just opted out and refused to use any fuel at all? He probably wouldn't get too far, now would he?

Breakfast should be eaten within two hours of waking up. Besides providing the body with energy, breakfast also provides a host of key vitamins and minerals that are otherwise harder to obtain throughout the day if missed at breakfast. We should always have a daily five of fruits and veggies, a key source of key nutrients. That is why it is so helpful to include fruits or veggies with breakfast for the body to absorb the proper level of these key nutrients each day.

The brain needs energy to work at its best. That is why breakfast is so vital to having a successful day. Breakfast restores glucose levels, an essential carbohydrate that is a must for proper brain function. If you want to be productive throughout your day, you must possess a positive mood—there's no getting around that. Negative thoughts cause the mind to wander, resulting in loss of concentration. There are studies that have shown that eating breakfast can improve memory and concentration. It can also make us happier and lower stress levels tremendously, resulting in a positive, action-filled day. Did you know that the brain under stress can lose volume? Yes, when a brain is under stress, the cells literally shrink. A brain cell must stay active for it to maintain connections with other neurons. These connections, called synapses, will disintegrate and disappear if cells do not use them to communicate. You see, without the proper nutrients, the brain is not functioning properly or firing on all cylinders. Your mood and energy are low and this directly affects how much of the brain your using daily.

Carbohydrates help to boost mood by releasing the feel-good chemical serotonin. Carbohydrates, also known as carbs, can give the body the necessary boost that it needs, if used correctly. If not used correctly, it will still give the body a major boost but will be followed by a shocking crash. This drastic lowering causes hostility, sleepiness, and depression (Medical News Today, "Serotonin Enhances Learning," https://1ref.us/1vj [accessed March 30, 2022]). The right plan is to feed your brain with a proper balance of carbohydrates, fats, and proteins. This will satisfy hormones, and by producing happy hormones, the byproduct is a very sharp mind. It is imperative for all individuals to learn, and continue to learn, about optimum food pairing. If this balance is ignored, the results are usually quite consistent: emotional ups and downs.

The balanced diet consists of a few must-haves to complete the circle of proper nutrition. Carbohydrates, for one, feed the brain and are its main source of energy. Proteins slow down the rate at which the carbs are consumed, stabilizing blood sugar levels. Insulin, a wonderful little hormone, drives blood sugar into the cells to prevent fats from breaking down, storing glucose for later use. Insulin is what allows the body to use sugar from carbs for energy. Fats boost feel-good hormones and help regulate blood chemistry. You see why there must be a balance; they all work together in perfect harmony.

Carbs, if they are not attached to fiber (white bread, white rice, white potatoes, white pasta, etc.), give bursts of energy but drastically plummet quickly thereafter (Healthline, "7 Foods That Drain Your Energy," https://1ref.us/1vk [accessed March 30, 2022]). When this occurs, you aren't receiving a steady supply of energy throughout your day. This will directly affect your concentration. A sugar high is simply just that: extreme hyperactivity, accompanied by inability to concentrate. Then when the sugar wears off, the body gets tired. To have the associated fiber is like having a good investment. The fiber causes a slow digestion of the sugar, resulting in your body receiving time-released bursts of energy throughout the day. So, I would strongly agree that it is far better to eat whole grains, brown rice, yams, whole wheat pastas, flax seeds, chia seeds, and all veggies that contain a good amount of fiber. Your brain will thank you.

The right amount of protein at the right time is so vital. Proteins are simply long chains of amino acids that are important molecules that we obtain through our diets. Protein is so critical, especially if you are trying to build muscle mass, have better neurological function, better digestion, naturally balance hormones, or maintain an upbeat mood. Protein is used by every single cell in our bodies (MedlinePlus, "Protein in a Diet," https://1ref.us/1vl [accessed March 30, 2022]). For instance, tyrosine the most important for energy because it produces dopamine and norepinephrine, helps humans keep focused, energized, and motivated. Tyrosine affects our mood by keeping the thyroid gland and its hormones active, regulating metabolism. Through this, stamina and mental clarity improve (WebMD, "Health Benefits of L-Tyrosine," https://1ref.us/1vm [accessed March 30, 2022]). The best sources for this amino acid are sunflower seeds, beans, bananas, almonds, fish, eggs, and soy products.

Amino acids are separate chemical compounds that can be found in a range of different foods. In the body, they are held together by peptide bonds. Diversity is key. Without enough diverse protein food choices, we run the risk of becoming deficient in certain amino acids. The side effects? Trouble building muscle, low energy levels, low concentration and memory, mood swings, unstable blood sugar levels and trouble maintaining or losing weight.

Fat is a macronutrient, and it is one of the main three that is used by the human body. The other two, of course, are carbohydrates and protein. Fat is a necessary part of our daily diets, especially those fatty acids that cannot be synthesized in the body from simpler constituents. There are two essential fatty acids in nutrition. One is linolenic acid which is the omega-3s and the other is linoleic acid which is the omega-6 fatty acid. The reason for the name omega-3 is because there are three varieties. The two that are vital for daily productivity are EPA which is eicospentaenoic acid and the other is DHA which is also known as docosapentaenoic acid. Both are essentials that elevate mood and increase emotional stability (NIH, "Omega-3 Fatty Acids EPA and DHA: Health Benefits Throughout Life," https://1ref.us/1wt [accessed May 10, 2022]). People who eat more foods that contain these fatty acids are generally healthier, mentally and physically, then those that don't. The omega-3 preserves overall cognitive function (awareness and perception). These fats are key components of nerve cell membranes that insulate the sheath around the nerve cell fibers that transmit signals in the brain. Omega-3 fats save the brain by preserving blood flow through all the tiny little blood vessels. Dietary consumption of these fatty acids, replacing saturated fats with unsaturated fats, significantly increases brain power and decreases the risk of cardiovascular disease. The same protein found in omega-3s is also found in dark leafy green vegetables, flaxseed, walnuts, and seaweed. These proteins produce neurotransmitters in vast proportions. Fats also serve as energy sources and as stores for energy in excess of what the body may need immediately.

Exercise

"In order for the brain to have clearness and strength of thought, retentive memory and mental power, the muscles of the body should have exercise a portion of each day" (White, "Proper Education," *The Signs of the Times*, April 29, 1875).

As we age, and as a result of daily stress on the body, the mind shrinks. Stress kills off neurons and decreases brain mass in excess of the rate of stress that the body endures on a daily basis. Luckily, we serve a strategic God that has put in place natural regenerative practices that can totally rejuvenate a deferred thought process. Yes, our thought process is affected greatly. As the number of neurons decrease, the number of synapses between neurons decreases as well, resulting in a slower thinking pattern or thought process. It was once thought that the body produces neurons in our younger years but slows to a halt as we reach adulthood—not so. One form of regeneration that has been discovered is known as adult hippocampal neurogenesis. This is an amazing form of neural circuit plasticity that causes the generation of new neurons in the dentate gyrus continuously over the course of a lifetime (Nature, https://1ref.us/1vn [accessed March 30, 2022]). Adult-born neurons show heightened synaptic plasticity during their maturation. They also account for about 10 percent of the overall granule cell population (Ibid.). The best part is that levels of neurogenesis are increased through simple natural interventions. Interventions such as learning, environmental enrichment, and exercise all play a vital role in positively effecting cognition and mood. When harnessed, these actions improve hippocampal function which is responsible for the consolidation of information from short-term memory to long-term memory as well as spatial memory used for navigation (Ibid.).

Now, whoever said that exercise isn't that important? It's not just important, it's vital to our functional existence. Ever since man has left the Garden of Eden, resulting from sin, life has been made hard. Man went from having an abundance of every natural food there was, to having to toil and till the ground in order to bring forth food. With this shift, the animal population was also affected, as in lions that were once vegetarians weren't so herbivorous anymore. So as the world changed, man's skills had to change along with it for survival. Man had to work extremely hard to produce anything, so exercise was life. Hunting, gathering, planting, herding, fighting, and escaping from anything that was life threatening was all in a day's work—very active lifestyles. To survive in this environment, the antediluvians had to know how to run, walk, balance, jump, crawl, climb, lift, carry, throw, and catch. Sounds like a lot of the structured movements we incorporate in our modern workout plans, right?! As we progressed as a people and civilizations were created, the need for physical exercise was used for different reasons. Civilizations rose and fell through war and conquest. Thus, physical fitness was then structuralized and imposed upon young men for the preparation of battle. The Babylonians, Assyrians, Egyptians, and Persians were all at the forefront of war preparation, but the Greeks and the Romans took it to another level. Their daily regiment consisted of jumping, crawling, climbing, lifting and carrying heavy objects, throwing, catching, running on uneven terrain, unarmed combat, and weapons training. Such ancient civilizations valued physical culture also for the use in sports. There are records of athletic competitions existing in ancient Egypt and in ancient Greece (Wikipedia, "History of Sport," https://1ref.us/1vo [accessed March 30, 2022]). These sporting events involved practical natural movements that, in those times, were used primarily for war prep. Physical fitness later evolved even more with the Greeks and Romans to the point that it was considered a necessary part of one's complete education. They began to value the idea of having a sound mind in a sound body. Physical culture, at that moment, rose to become a means to an end, no longer just a practical necessity.

As we moved into the Dark Ages, things changed a little—well maybe a lot. The Middle Ages brought with it very chaotic times, with several successions of kingdoms and empires, invasion after invasion, and way too many plagues. The spread of Catholicism was on the rise, and from their influence, the focus of one's life was shifted more towards preparing for the afterlife. The body at this point was seen as sinful and unimportant; it was the soul that was the major focal point then. Education was tied to the church in a major way then and was focused more on cultivating the mind rather than the body. The evidence of this choice was made very clear during this time with such poor living conditions, plagues running rampant, and the overall decreasing physical ability in the population as a whole. For optimum health, one must work for a good balance of mind, body, and spirit. There is not one without the other; they all work together in perfect harmony to create good health. As the world entered the Renaissance era, interests begin to shift more towards the body once again. Special schools began to pop up, prompting the study of the body, anatomy, health, biology, and physical education (Wikipedia, "History of Physical Training and Fitness," https://1ref.us/1vp [accessed March 30, 2022]). It was during this time that games and sports were fully analyzed and suggestions were created for better treating injuries and for quicker recovery times. Gymnastics was created during this period. I would deem it safe to say that through this era, physical fitness began to take on a life of its own, a culture was emerging (*Smithsonian Magazine*, "A History of Gymnastics," https://1ref.us/1vq [accessed March 30, 2022]). Over the course of this era, advancements in the areas of study of the human body increased significantly and carried us forward into the industrial revolution.

The industrial revolution marked a significant transition in our societies. The move from manual production methods to machine-based production, created the manufacturing era. With this great shift, around 1760, came a total change in social, economic, and cultural trends. It changed the way people worked, lived, moved, and learned (Britannica, "Industrial Revolution," https://1ref.us/1vr [accessed March 30, 2022]). As people became more stationary, physical exertion decreased more and more. This resulted in declining health due to increased stress, poor eating habits, lack of fresh air and sun, and poor blood flow. Thus, the dawn of intentional physical exercise began to arise. Dudley Allen Sargent (1849–1924), considered to be the founder of physical education in the United States, created the universal test for strength, speed, and endurance in 1902 (Wikipedia, "Dudley Allen Sargent," https://1ref.us/1vs [accessed March 30, 2022]). He once quoted that "Without solid physical education programs, people would become fat, deformed, and clumsy" (MovNat, "The History of Physical Fitness," https://1ref.us/1vt [accessed March 30, 2022]). If we look at the epidemic that this country has been facing for years, I would agree that he was right on the money. That's why his work was centered around incorporating physical education into our daily routines. Edmond Desbonnet and Bernarr Macfadden are considered to be the precursors of the health and fitness industry as we know it (Art of Manliness, "The History of Physical Fitness," https://1ref.us/1vu [accessed March 30, 2022]). They both sought to make physical education and fitness fashionable through magazine publications and by opening chains of fitness clubs (Ibid.). Fast-forward to the twenty-first century and this cultural trend still remains, but not only that, it is now a 24.2-billion-dollar industry.

Incorporating daily exercise into one's lifestyle doesn't have to be that complicated; it's quite simple, actually. If you join a gym and actually stick to a routine of working out regularly each week, then that's awesome—great job! For those that don't have a gym membership, all hope isn't gone. If you don't have the finances or the space for all these fancy exercise DVDs or equipment, it's OK! All anyone really needs is a floor or access to the outdoors. The secret is creating the habit of incorporating physical activity into our daily lives. If you have a long driveway and you always get the mail as your pulling into the drive way, here is a thought: go ahead and drive to your house and walk to the mail box; it's that simple. Change your daily routines and you will change your life. Instead of opening the door and letting the dogs into the backyard, actually take them for a walk two to three times a week. If you're watching TV, do 100 pushups or sit ups or crunches or leg lifts or plank. The key is to do something, and the more you do it, the less hard it gets to motivate yourself to engage in physical activity regularly. I, for one, have a pull-up bar that I have placed across a doorway in my house, and every time I pass under it to go back upstairs, I have to do ten pull-ups. I have resistance bands next to my desk in my home office so when I'm writing or doing research, I take a break and do a set. I have dumbbells under my bed so that I can do a quick workout before bed. I have an app on my phone that is used for doing squats; I hate doing leg workouts, so it structures the workout for me which motivates me to finish. One ritual that we have created as a family is to go for nice walks on Sabbath afternoon either on a nature trail or by a beautiful body of water. Hopefully you are now getting the idea. If you want to change your daily routine, keep it in your sights always.

Water

> And he was sore athirst, and called on the LORD, and said, Thou hast given this great deliverance into the hand of thy servant: and now shall I die for thirst, and fall into the hand of

the uncircumcised? But God clave an hollow place that was in the jaw, and there came water thereout; and when he had drunk, his spirit came again, and he revived. (Judges 15:18–19)

Water is a clear and nearly colorless chemical substance. It covers about 71 percent of the earth's surface (Wikipedia, "Water," https://1ref.us/1vv [accessed March 31, 2022]). Water is the main substance that makes up all of the earth's streams, lakes, oceans, and rivers. It is also the main fluid for all living organisms. Its chemical formula, as we all know, is H2O, meaning its molecule has one oxygen and two hydrogen atoms. They are held together by a covalent bond, which is a chemical bond that involves the sharing of electron pairs between atoms.

Water has many properties that make it vital for all life on earth. All life is based on organic compounds, and water allows these compounds to react in ways that ultimately allow replication. Replication is simple: Let's say cells, given a suitable environment, begin to replicate by cell division. Water is also vital to the body's many metabolic processes, such as the conversion of food/fuel to energy.

> In catabolism, water is used to break bonds in order to generate smaller molecules (e.g., glucose, fatty acids, and amino acids to be used for fuels for energy use or other purposes). Without water, these particular metabolic processes could not exist. Water is fundamental to photosynthesis and respiration. Photosynthetic cells use the sun's energy to split off water's hydrogen from oxygen. Hydrogen is combined with CO_2 (absorbed from air or water) to form glucose and release oxygen. All living cells use such fuels and oxidize the hydrogen and carbon to capture the sun's energy and reform water and CO_2 in the process (cellular respiration). (Ibid., [accessed March 31, 2022])

Drink water every day. At least eight glasses, or sixty-four ounces, of water are needed for the body each day (Healthline, "How Much Water Should You Drink?" https://1ref.us/1vw [accessed March 31, 2022]). The best kinds of water to drink are natural spring waters which are bottled at the source or artesian and spring waters that are bottled off-site. These waters tend to still possess the vital minerals that are needed for all the functions of the body. If we take a look at all the bottled waters around today, most are simply tap water that has been cleaned up. Cleaned up, unfortunately, means that it has been stripped of all the minerals that make water such a powerhouse. Usually these waters have been either purified (treated, processed, disinfected with chlorine and fluoride added), distilled (vaporized—stripped of all minerals), or gone through reverse osmosis (forced through membranes to remove pollutants and minerals—usually acidic). These waters lack the essential minerals that are conducive to good health. Mineral deficiency can lead to migraines, high blood pressure, insulin resistance, heartbeat irregularities, or even constipation.

Water is most effective if drank at the proper times. If you drink two glasses of water in the morning, right after you wake up, it helps to activate your internal organs. One glass of water, thirty minutes before a meal, aids in digestion. One glass of water while taking a bath helps with high blood pressure, and one glass before going to bed helps to avoid heart attacks or strokes. This is wonderful and all, but if you are not drinking any water hardly ever, it's best to just get in the habit of drinking water first then advance to strategizing your water intake. The best way to create a habit of drinking more water throughout your day is just to always have water with you. My mother always taught me to drink a lot of water; she would always say, "Keep water with you at all times." So, wherever I go, I always have a bottle of water with me. Even if I'm just going to the store or to take the trash to the dump, I have a bottle of water by my side. If you want to change your routines, always keep that which you would like to do differently in sight. Also, my wife and I did some reading on how harmful plastic bottles can be. So, one day, we were in a store and saw glass water bottles; we purchased one for each of us and have never looked back since. Drinking water out of a glass water bottle is not only safer, but the taste of the water remains intact the entire time. We love our glass bottles, and you can find them wherever we go. We strongly suggest the use of glass water bottles in everyone's pursuit of increased water intake.

Sunlight

"Truly the light is sweet, and a pleasant thing it is for the eyes to behold the sun" (Eccles. 11:7).

> Nature and revelation alike testify of God's love. Our Father in heaven is the source of life, of wisdom, and of joy. Look at the wonderful and beautiful things of nature. Think of their marvelous adaptation to the needs and happiness, not only of man, but of all living creatures. The sunshine and the rain, that gladden and refresh the earth, the hills and seas and plains, all speak to us of the Creator's love. It is God who supplies the daily needs of all His creatures. (White, *Steps to Christ*, p. 9)

Sunlight is an electromagnetic radiation given off by the sun, and it is wonderful. When the rays from the sun shine through completely unobstructed by the clouds, we experience sunshine. It is this combination of bright light and radiant heat that remains constant fuel for nearly all life on earth. We are so lucky to serve such a strategic God. Everything God has created has so many different benefits for us. Getting enough sunlight is so important, in so many ways. While too much of the sun's warm rays may not be the best thing for the skin, the right balance is the key. No sunlight is simply detrimental to our overall health. Sunlight is absorbed through the skin and creates vitamin D, an essential to good bone health. Sunlight is also a purifier, it brings to the surface the bodies impurities (germs, toxins) in order to flush it out of the system. This can be beneficial in the prevention of cancer, the spreading of viruses and can increase vigor. Sunlight can also play a key role in living a productive life. As we have been learning, one of the biggest enemies to our progress is our moods. Sunlight can boost and elevate mood by increasing our serotonin levels. The effects of serotonin are light-induced and are triggered by the sunlight (Healthline, "Benefits of Sunlight." https://1ref.us/1vx [accessed March 31, 2022]). The sunlight enters the eye and cues different areas of the retina which, in turn, triggers the release of serotonin. If you want to relieve anxiety and reduce depression this is the natural way to go. An easy way to get more sunlight in your life, choose more outdoor activities. When you exercise, do your routine outside in the sun some days. Eat lunch outside as much as you can and follow it with a nice walk. God has given us all the keys to happiness in this life and they are all free to use. The very definition of sunshine is cheerfulness and happiness (Google, "Sunshine," https://1ref.us/1vy [accessed March 31, 2022]).

> Above all things, parents should surround their children with an atmosphere of cheerfulness, courtesy, and love. A home where love dwells and where it finds expression in looks, in words, in acts, is a place where angels delight to dwell. Parents, let the sunshine of love, cheer, and happy content enter your own hearts, and let its sweet influence pervade the home. Manifest a kindly, forbearing spirit, and encourage the same in your children, cultivating all those graces that will brighten the home life. The atmosphere thus created will be to the children what air and sunshine are to the vegetable world, promoting health and vigor of mind and body. (White, *The Adventist Home*, p. 426)

Temperance

> And this I do for the gospel's sake, that I might be partaker thereof with you. Know ye not that they which run in a race run all, but one receiveth the prize? So run, that ye may obtain. And every man that striveth for the mastery is temperate in all things. Now they do it to obtain a corruptible crown; but we an incorruptible. I therefore so run, not as uncertainly; so fight I, not as one that beateth the air: But I keep under my body, and bring it into subjection [control]: lest that by any means, when I have preached to others, I myself should be a castaway. (1 Cor. 9:23–27)

Oftentimes when people hear the word temperance, they immediately associate it with the consumption of alcohol. This, in fact, is largely a result of the temperance movement of the 1920s which ultimately led to the ever-famous prohibition which banned the production, importation, transportation, and overall sale of alcohol (Britannica, "Prohibition," https://1ref.us/1vz [accessed March 31, 2022]). By no means is this a true representation of what true temperance is, though. While this may have been a noble pursuit to better society, it lacked the one seraphic nuance that could connect it to our divine Creator. It lacked the opportunity for choice!

> The world is given to self-indulgence. Errors and fables abound. Satan's snares for destroying souls are multiplied. All who would perfect holiness in the fear of God must learn the lessons of temperance and self-control. The appetites and passions must be held in subjection to the higher powers of the mind. This self-discipline is essential to that mental strength and spiritual insight which will enable us to understand and to practice the sacred truths of God's word. For this reason temperance finds its place in the work of preparation for Christ's second coming. (White, *The Desire of Ages*, pp. 100–101)

"In order to preserve health, temperance in all things is necessary,—temperance in labor, temperance in eating and drinking" (White, *Healthful Living*, p. 68).

"True temperance teaches us to dispense entirely with everything hurtful, and to use judiciously that which is healthful" (White, *The Faith I Live By*, p. 231).

Many people think that moderation is the key to a healthy lifestyle, but it's a bit more than that. To practice true temperance, oftentimes it requires of us to abstain from things that are unhealthy for us all together. Heroin is a horrible addictive drug; you wouldn't go and tell a teenager, "If done in moderation, everything will be OK," now would you? You see, God has blessed us with the power of discernment that is most powerful when influenced by the Holy

Spirit. He has blessed us with the ability to learn about the unknown in order to protect ourselves and the ones we love and hold so dear. God says that "My people are destroyed for lack of knowledge" (Hosea 4:6). We must become educated in the art of creating healthful habits and come to know what must be used in moderation and what things are best to just be left alone.

Temperance is the essence of a beautiful lifelong walk with God, for we can't navigate through this life on our own. We must rely wholeheartedly on our Creator and His Holy Spirit to guide us along our journey. Temperance is the key for us to begin manifesting this powerful awareness, awareness that is needed in order for us to recognize a divine task, tailor-made just for us, sent to us by God whenever that time may be. Our bodies are temples that have been bought and paid for with a substantial price. Remember our mission, it's the same now as it has always been since our first parents left the Garden of Eden. Be unto Him a proper vessel that can be used by God to finish His work. Fulfill God's purpose.

"God had called the son of Zacharias to a great work, the greatest ever committed to men. In order to accomplish this work, he must have the Lord to work with him. And the Spirit of God would be with him if he heeded the instruction of the angel" (White, *Lift Him Up*, p. 363).

> John was to go forth as Jehovah's messenger, to bring to men the light of God. He must give a new direction to their thoughts. He must impress them with the holiness of God's requirements, and their need of His perfect righteousness. Such a messenger must be holy. He must be a temple for the indwelling Spirit of God. In order to fulfill his mission, he must have a sound physical constitution, and mental and spiritual strength. Therefore it would be necessary for him to control the appetites and passions. He must be able so to control all his powers that he could stand among men as unmoved by surrounding circumstances as the rocks and mountains of the wilderness. (Ibid.)

Temperance is simply self-discipline in all things; self-discipline is simply a choice, and we make dozens of choices every single day. "The basis of a right character in the future man is made firm by habits of strict temperance ..." (White, *The Adventist Home*, p. 258). The sum of each day compounds upon itself to form our paths, and it is our paths that ultimately hold the key to our futures. The question is "Will it be a future with God at the center of it"? Or will it be the latter? The choice is ours.

Air

> Air, air, the precious boon of heaven which all may have, will bless you with its invigorating influence if you will not refuse it entrance. Welcome it, cultivate a love for it, and it will prove a precious soother of the nerves. Air must be in constant circulation to be kept pure. The influence of pure, fresh air is to cause the blood to circulate healthfully through the system. It refreshes the body and tends to render it strong and healthy, while at the same time its influence is decidedly felt upon the mind, imparting a degree of composure and serenity. It excites the appetite, and renders the digestion of food more perfect, and induces sound and sweet sleep. (White, *Testimonies for the Church*, vol. 1, p. 702)

Air is the most precious gift given to all living organisms. We can go weeks without food and even days without water, but without air we would barely last minutes. The current record for someone being able to hold their breath now is twenty-four minutes and three seconds (Wired, "What It Takes to Hold Your Breath," https://1ref.us/1w0 [accessed April 1, 2022]). Now mind you that this was a person that trained for months to be able to accomplish this. The average person can barely hold their breath for thirty to forty seconds without gasping for air. The body needs a constant circulation of pure, clean fresh air. The body and its 100 trillion cells need nourishment through each breath that we take, and we take about 22,000 of those a day (Canadian Lung Association, "Breathing," https://1ref.us/1w1 [accessed April 1, 2022]). The heart uses blood to drop off carbon dioxide to the lungs for elimination, then it receives fresh oxygen and delivers it to every cell in the body.

Fresh air has many benefits that affect health, mental ability, healing, and even energy levels. Fresh air increases serotonin levels in our bodies, which aid in proper brain function and elevating mood. Without a consistent flow of fresh air, our bodies tend to begin to deteriorate faster. We become sluggish, have headaches and a host of other aches and pains. When we get sick, we release all sorts of poisons into the air and without proper ventilation, we just keep inhaling and exhaling bad air that is not conducive to good health. Quite a few of our modern houses have such poor ventilation, and we constantly—without notice—breathe in and exhale stale air. Think about all the hospitals that you visit, and it has that ever-so-distinguishing odor that keeps you alert as to where you are. We, as a society, have forgotten and even never learned God's basic health solutions that have been around for centuries. When you cut your finger and put a bandage on it, and when you take that bandage off, what does your injury look like? Does it look like it has begun to heal or does it look even worse? Usually it's all moist and wrinkled, and sometimes even infected, right?! Why is that? It's because it has been kept from fresh air. Air is God's healing agent. Most illnesses that are prolonged to heal are due to lack of proper fresh air circulation, because good air isn't allowed to enter the body for the oxygen to aid in healing from the inside out (Phantom Screens, "Getting Fresh Air Part 1," https://1ref.us/1w2 [accessed April 1, 2022]). We can alleviate a lot of life's ailments with the simple habitual exposure to good, unpolluted fresh air.

We should make a conscious effort to open windows in our homes daily. But keep in mind that air is a sluggish gas and oftentimes needs assistance to be able to circulate. I often use clean fans and an air purifier to aid in purification and circulation. We should also exercise in the fresh air more to improve health faster. Exercise is good but when done inside all the time—like in an unventilated gym or home—it can become a bit counterproductive. Deep breathing of fresh air induced by exercise works well in the overcoming of fear, developing courage, and strengthening the nervous system. Pure fresh air is so vital and so important that God made it possible for our bodies to breath constantly uninterrupted all day without any attention needed by us. It is God's purpose for us to breath pure fresh air throughout our entire existence.

Rest

> Remember the sabbath day, to keep it holy. Six days shalt thou labour, and do all thy work: but the seventh day is the sabbath of the Lord thy God: in it thou shalt not do any work, thou, nor thy son, nor thy daughter, thy manservant, nor thy maidservant, nor thy cattle, nor thy stranger that is within thy gates: for in six days the Lord made heaven and earth, the sea, and all that in them is, and rested the seventh day: wherefore the Lord blessed the sabbath day, and hallowed it. (Exod. 20:8–11)

Rest is so important that God, during Creation, set aside a whole day for us to rest. God worked for six days, creating what we know now to be earth, but He rested the seventh day. Now why did He see it necessary to rest for a day? Better yet, why did He see it necessary to rest at the end of each day after He was finished with His tasks for each day? Have you ever wondered?

God says: "Come unto me, all ye that labour and are heavy laden, and I will give you rest. Take my yoke upon you, and learn of me; for I am meek and lowly in heart: and ye shall find rest unto your souls. For my yoke is easy, and my burden is light" (Matt. 11:28–30).

God considers rest to be a vital source of power generation. After each day of creating, God would sit back and say it is good (Gen. 1:4–31). This implies that He sat back and rested after each day of work to build strength for the next day. On the seventh day, He rested completely and blessed that day, meaning that day was to be separate from the rest. "And God blessed the seventh day, and sanctified it: because that in it he had rested from all his work which God created and made" (Gen. 2:3). Now, we know God didn't need to build strength; this was more so setting an example for His children. By taking this day off, spending time communing with God through study, fellowshipping with family and friends, enjoying good Christ-centered music, it builds faith. It takes faith to completely let go of all the stress and worries and trust that God will take care of everything. This is what God's intention was for this day, a day for us to spend time getting to know our Father. It is through this day that we truly express our love to Him, because it is only by choice that we keep this day holy. If your father could only spend one day a week with you and it was every Tuesday, but you decide to always show up on Wednesday and called him saying "I'm here to visit," knowing that he couldn't get there, how do you think that would make him feel? He would be heartbroken, right? God created this day for reflection. Reflection on how good He has been to us each week. Reflection on how He gave His Son's life to save us from our sins. There is a reverence that we give to God by honoring this day.

Besides the spiritual aspect, rest is just so important to our overall health. The right amount of sleep is essential to optimum functionality and a healthy lifestyle. The body must be allowed time to heal and reabsorb natural forces that it has exhausted through work, exercise, mental strain, and so on. It is impossible for us to grow without the aid of rest, physically or intellectually. Without sleep, the body is unable to recharge itself adequately. Irritability is increased and creativity, concentration, and efficiency all suffer. Nowadays, everyone is on the go so much, trying to gain so much and, in all actuality, we are losing because of lack of rest. No time for reading, relaxation, quiet reflection, practicing, memorizing, leisure. You tell me, how can someone grow without these? The true Christian walk is constant growth each and every day through constant communion with the Father. The only way we get more rest is by increasing our faith in Him. "Peace I leave with you, my peace I give unto you: not as the world giveth, give I unto you. Let not your heart be troubled, neither let it be afraid" (John 14:27). So, rest!

Trust

> Day by day we are all to be trained, disciplined, and educated for usefulness in this life. Only one day at a time—think of this. One day is mine. I will in this one day do my best. I will use my talent of speech to be a blessing to some other one, a helper, a comforter, an example which the Lord my Savior shall approve. I will exercise myself in patience, kindness, forbearance, that the Christian virtues may be developed in me today. (White, *In Heavenly Places*, p. 227)

> Every morning dedicate yourself, soul, body, and spirit, to God. Establish habits of devotion and trust more and more in your Saviour. You may believe with all confidence that the Lord Jesus loves you and wishes you to grow up to His stature of character. He wishes you to grow in His love, to increase and strengthen in all the fullness of divine love. Then you will gain a knowledge of the highest value for time and for eternity. (White, *Mind, Character, and Personality*, vol. 1, p. 15)

What is trust? Trust is "[f]irm belief in the reliability, truth, ability, or strength of someone or something" (Lexico, "Trust," https://1ref.us/1w3 [accessed April 1, 2022]). At least that's the way the dictionary defines "trust." What is divine trust? You see the definition in the dictionary leaves the implication that the belief is factored and strengthened by the tangible, which is fair because we as humans are accustomed to using our senses to factor our body's response to any given situation. This is what I call phase one trust. We are so lucky to serve a God that is all knowing (because He created us) and prepared the way for us to move towards what we all need—and that's divine trust. Trust that is based on faith.

"Now FAITH is the substance of things hoped for, the evidence of things not seen" (Heb. 11:1, capitalization supplied by the author).

This is phase two trust. "But without faith it is impossible to please him: for he that cometh to God must believe that he is, and that he is a rewarder of them that diligently seek him" (Heb. 11:6). This trust is built over time spent getting to know our Creator. Since we are human and we use our senses most of the time to make decisions, God understood this and sent us help. By studying the Word (the Bible) we get to know who God is through something tangible. The more we seek Him, the stronger our faith and belief in Him grows. Let's say all summer long, every time you watched TV, you saw a soda commercial for your favorite soda. With its catchy jingle and crazy visual antics, you found yourself humming the jingle randomly and often unconsciously. Not only that, but you also started consuming way more than the normal amount of this soda that you love so much. Why is that? Well, your senses were manipulated and the want for this soft drink was increased without your permission, it was embedded into your subconscious, making you crave that object.

This is how we must be with our Creator, except He waits respectfully for you to give Him permission. To seek Him wholeheartedly, we are embedding Him into our subconscious so that to exemplify faith becomes but second nature. The tangible isn't needed for you to know who you serve because you already know, feel, and trust Him wholeheartedly. Now don't get me wrong, you always need to seek God through study that is never ending, and that is the beauty of it. There is endless room for growth—the true Christian walk! What I am saying is that after you have been doing it for a while, just as you become mentally and physically fit, you will get in divine shape to trust in God no matter what the circumstances are.

"Trust in the Lord with all thine heart; and lean not unto thine own understanding. In all thy ways acknowledge him, and he shall direct thy paths. Be not wise in thine own eyes: fear the Lord, and depart from evil" (Prov. 3:5–7).

Chapter 4

The Antediluvian World

How We Must Learn from Our True History

At the end of a prolonged busy week of work, you finally get to enter your humble abode with a new zeal for life. A sudden rush of excitement surges through your entire being as you realize that it's Friday, and you are at the beginning of your much-coveted weekend. Better yet, you are now at the beginning of what some refer to as Sabbath rest. You plop down onto your favorite couch. "Only for a moment" you ever so graciously but adamantly recite to yourself several times, while subsequently sinking deeper and deeper into those ever so soft down/feather cushions. As your mind clears and your body begins to unwind, YOU WAKE UP!! Wondering how you could have ever fallen asleep and slightly stressing thinking of the chores that need to be done before morning, you sit up slowly; confusion begins to increase as you realize your couch isn't under you anymore. You quickly turn around, only to find that everything that concerned you thirty seconds ago is completely miniscule in comparison to what you are facing right now. Mouth opened wide in complete awe and disbelief of what you are witnessing right before your eyes at this very moment, you gaze out at this beautiful city surrounding you, wondering if you somehow skipped everything and went straight to heaven.

Streets paved with gold, beautiful architecture all over, buildings with huge marble columns, and grand walls with every type of fruit you could imagine draped over the top. Crystal clear water flowing through the entire city by way of rivers, springs, lakes, and magnificent, captivating waterfalls. Flying machines resembling animals zipping back and forth, harnessing the ever-present power flowing throughout the entire city; everywhere the eye can see is a vision of pure grandeur. Wait! Wait! Wait! This is beginning to resemble another story, isn't it? Starting to sound a little like Atlantis the lost city, right? The one that was said to be majestically ancient as well as highly advanced (i.e., mentally and technologically). *Hmm*! The story of Atlantis was created by Plato a Greek philosopher, and he told the story around 360 BC (Wikipedia, "Atlantis," https://1ref.us/1w4 [accessed April 4, 2022]). The story is about a moral and very spiritual people that lived in a utopian civilization that was highly advanced. They became greedy, petty, and morally bankrupt. The way Plato tells the story, the gods grew angry because the people lost their way and chose immoral pursuits. As punishment for these continual acts of betrayal, it is said that the gods sent "one terrible night of fire and earthquakes" that caused Atlantis to sink into the sea (National Geographic, "Atlantis," https://1ref.us/1w5 [accessed April 4, 2022]). That's very peculiar in light of another story that shares many similarities with this one but had a completely opposite ending. This story had a prophet named Noah that warned this ancient, intelligent, advanced civilization for several years—120 to be exact—that their end was coming because God was unpleased with their wicked and corrupt actions (Gen. 6:3). Their society had also become greedy, petty, and morally bankrupt. Notice one key point though: God always gives sufficient warning for redemption before destruction comes. In the first story, destruction came without any notice. No chance for redemption, in other words. What was the purpose of it all?

The striking resemblance of these two stories definitely poses the question of the source of Plato's inspiration for the great tale of Atlantis. Some argue that the tale is solely based on the ancient Minoan civilization and that the destructing force that ended their days was that of an eruption of Thera on Santorini located in the Aegean. Others believe that it was but a beautifully constructed bit of fiction to illustrate the glory of Plato's magnificent Athens. Well, how about this scenario? Plato started revealing this story around 360 BC. We also know that Plato enjoyed traveling all over the world just like one of his ancestors who spent ten years of his life—to be precise—traveling the world. (Wikipedia, "Solon," https://1ref.us/1w6 [accessed April 4, 2022]) Solon and his brother Dropides were Plato's ancestors, six generations removed. Solon was a poet, an Athenian statesman, and a lawmaker. He is particularly known for his legislative efforts against political, economic, and moral decline—how ironic (Ibid. [accessed April 4, 2022]). In his youth, Solon began to endeavor in commerce by necessity. His father's estate was severely impaired due to excessive philanthropic efforts and funds were very lack. Solon was ashamed to receive any help from friends especially those that had witnessed the consistent generosity of his family. So, he embarked upon a journey that would take him far away from Athens. He used commerce as the vehicle to take him, but the journey was not as much about money as it was about the experiences and the knowledge that would be gained. It was on the Canopian shore that Solon began and continued to converse philosophy and history with some of the most intelligent priests and leaders that Egypt had to offer. There were also Jews in Egypt during this time as well as in many of the other cities in which Solon frequented. Could it be, quite possibly, that an Egyptian Jew or an Egyptian or any other individual that had an accurate true account of the ancient world handed down from generation to generation told Solon of the story of the antediluvians who roamed the earth before the great flood, in vivid detail? Egyptians were said to have had direct contact with antediluvians from the ancient world (The Torah, "Antediluvian Knowledge," https://1ref.us/1wu [accessed May 10, 2022]). In hindsight, this could offer much explanation to the advanced architectural skill of the Egyptians. Solon heard this great story of the antediluvians over and over again and it resonated with him. For someone with such a passion for reversing the decline of political, economic, and moral values, he gravitated to the story's core and began to structure a story of his own that he could use for his cause to illustrate the consequences of one's actions if not rooted in morality. Incidentally, this is the initial purpose of the story of Atlantis. We also now know that many of the early workings of Solon possessed many interpolations. Many as such performed by Plato himself.

The use of these stories in Greece would, of course, mean the need for adaptation of them to fit into Greek ideology. Think about it for a moment. Plato was a philosopher. He was probably always looking for new inspirations to create an advanced way of thinking, by providing new stories to help steer his audience in the direction that he wanted them to go. Plato is said to have had a heavy influence on modern Christianity in the Western world as well. For someone to accomplish this, they would have to have spent many hours conversing with non-Greek individuals or reviewing the work of people that had already possessed many of these ideologies also because these concepts pre-date Plato. So, the story of Atlantis, as well as a host of Plato's philosophies, had to have been influenced by some greater concept of antiquity. Of course, Greece, because of its stature, anything coming out of this world leader was immediately projected unto all the world as new or innovative.

The story of Atlantis is often viewed as being fake, creative, fictional, even impossible by some. Which is all true in a sense! The story was adapted to better serve its audience. Plato replaced God with Greek deities and simply added more destructing forces besides just a flood to be the cause of the antediluvian's early demise (drama). He added in beliefs and ancient practices picked up from his travels and his ancestor's travels and blended them with his own philosophies to create the story of Atlantis and many of his other concepts. The fact of the matter is simply this: The people that this story is pertaining to were real. They existed before the flood and after the flood. We are all descendants of these magnificent beings; we are all descendants of greatness! Not of monkeys or apes or tadpoles that eventually turned into cavemen or whatever nonsense is floating around these days. #Greatness.

Knowledge has decreased since the antediluvian age, with each succeeding generation less and less aware because of sin. The people that roamed this earth before the flood received their instruction directly from our infinite Creator. God, who created this great earth, instilled His infinite knowledge upon these great people. There was no lack for wisdom on any subject pertaining to existing in this world. The antediluvians lived for hundreds of years and passed down this knowledge from generation to generation. They were blessed to be able to walk and learn from the firstborn Adam himself. Can you imagine the information that was conversed through this entire age? The antediluvians had exceptionally rare powers for planning and an even greater aptitude for the flawless execution of these plans. God bestowed upon them great gifts in all areas of their lives, and they used them all for the glorification of self (White, *Spiritual Gifts,* Vol. 4a, 121.2, https://1ref.us/1wv [accessed May 10, 2022]).

> How did man gain his knowledge of how to devise? From the Lord, by studying the formation and habits of different animals. Every animal is a lesson book, and form the use they make of their bodies and the weapons provided them, men have learned to make apparatus for every kind of work. If men could only know how many arts have been lost to our world, they would not talk so fluently of the dark ages. Could they have seen how God once worked through His human subjects, they would speak with less confidence of the arts of the antediluvian world. (White, *Letters and Manuscripts*, vol. 11)

> More was lost in the flood, in many ways, than men today know. Looking upon the world, God saw that the intellect He had given man was perverted, that the imagination of his heart was evil and that continually. God had given these men knowledge. He had given them valuable ideas, that they might carry out His plan. But the Lord saw that those whom He designed should possess wisdom, tact, and judgment, were using every quality of the mind to glorify self. By the waters of the flood, He blotted this long-lived race from the earth, and with them perished the knowledge they had used only for evil. When the earth was re-peopled, the Lord trusted His wisdom more sparingly to men, giving them only the ability they would need in carrying out His great plan. (Ibid.)

The antediluvians were giants three times the size of modern-day man (Sealing Time Ministries, https://1ref.us/1w7 [accessed April 4, 2022]). The tools we use today to plan and execute such wonderful endeavors, they didn't need. They could do it all in their minds and with their exceptional strength. Look at all the ancient artifacts that have been found that scientists have no explanation as to how it could have been conceived or constructed then and are unable to find anyone that can reproduce it in present day.

> There perished in the flood greater inventions of art and human skill than the world knows of today. The arts destroyed were more than the boasted arts of today. The great gifts with which God had endowed man were perfected. There was gold and silver in abundance, and men were constantly seeking to exceed their fellow men in devices. The result was that violence was upon the earth. The Lord was forgotten. This long lived race were constantly devising how they might institute a war with the universe of heaven and gain possession of Eden. (White, *Letters and Manuscripts*, vol. 13)

> When men talk of the improvements that are made in higher education, they are aping the inhabitants of the Noachic world. They are yielding to the temptation of Satan to eat of the tree of knowledge, of which God has said, "Ye shall not eat of it, lest ye die." [Genesis 3:3.] God gave men a trial, and the result was the destruction of the world by a flood. In this age of the world's history there are teachers and students who suppose that their advancement in knowledge supersedes the knowledge of God, and their cry is, "Higher education." They consider that they have greater knowledge that the greatest Teacher the world has ever known. (Ibid.)

We didn't evolve from a weak existence to what we are now but more so we have finally evolved from the significant decline in our human ability as a result of sin. We have only advanced so much in the past seventy years because of the dawn of industrialization and the invention of computers. Computers completely modeled after the human brain, might I add. Here's a thought, imagine being able to utilize 100 percent of your brain (your living computer). What could be accomplished! Oh, and if you had almost 1,000 years in which to perfect your skills to fulfill your purpose for being here, oh the possibilities. The antediluvians had time plus full functionality of their entire bodies. You do the calculations as to what had to have come into existence during their reign over this earth and how they failed miserably to fulfill God's will with such power. This leaves the question: Why did it take a great flood to wipe from the face of the earth this long-lived people, leaving only clues for us to find so that we can still witness how generous our God really was and still is? This generation had to be extremely powerful for it to take something of this magnitude to render the consequences of their actions. All other occurrences in the Bible where punishment was rendered, the punishment was controlled and contained to a general area—not the entire world. That's why God promised to never flood the entire earth again, because it wouldn't be needed with the significant decline in the succeeding generations. That is, of course, until the second coming at which time the world will be consumed by fire because the days are becoming more and more as in the time of Noah (Matt. 24:37–39).

Degenerated from Lightness to Debasing Sins— "We have the history of the antediluvians, and of the cities of the plain, whose course of conduct degenerated from lightness and frivolity to debasing sins that called down the wrath of God in a most dreadful destruction, in order to rid the earth of the curse of their contaminating influence. Inclination and passion bore sway over reason. Self was their god, and the knowledge of the Most High was nearly obliterated through the selfish indulgence of corrupt passions" (White, *Letters and Manuscripts*, vol. 11).

Perverted What Was Lawful— "The sin of the antediluvians was in perverting that which in itself was lawful. They corrupted God's gifts by using them to minister to their selfish desires. The indulgence of appetite and base passion made their imaginations altogether corrupt. The antediluvians were slaves of Satan, led and controlled by him" (White, *Letters and Manuscripts*, vol. 7).

Corrupted through Perverted Appetite— "The inhabitants of the Noachian world were destroyed because they were corrupted through the indulgence of perverted appetite" (White, *Testimonies for the Church*, vol. 3, p. 162).

Worshipped Self-Indulgence Fostered Crime— "They worshipped selfish indulgence—eating, drinking, merry-making—and resorted to acts of violence and crime if their desires and passions were interfered with. In the days of Noah the overwhelming majority was opposed to the truth and enamored with a tissue of falsehoods. The land was filled with violence. War, crime, murder was the order of the day. Just so will it be before Christ's second coming" (White, *Letters and Manuscripts*, vol. 7).

Just as Cain had to live with the remanence of sin, having to stare at the gate to Eden's bliss while he had to toil daily just to live, begrudgingly turning a stern eye towards the Creator with his self-righteous view of what life was supposed to be like on this earth for him, he grew angrier and more arrogant. This is the spirit that Cain passed down from generation to generation—the spirit that led to this once brilliant and beautiful race's corrupted view of what their purpose in this life truly was to be. They fixed their minds on the things of this earth rather than the holy things of their Creator. Their arrogance and hatred grew to such an astounding rate that they planned to go to war with the very One who gave them life. Any time you fight against God, who is responsible for your existence, you are simply expressing self-contempt. For it is when you are in tune with your Creator that you are at your very best and most happy self.

Once again it all comes down to one thing: purpose. "For the love of money is the root of all evil: which while some coveted after, they have erred from the faith, and pierced themselves through with many sorrows. But thou, O man of God, flee these things; and follow after righteousness, godliness, faith, love, patience, meekness" (1 Tim. 6:10–11). These are the true representations of our Creator. These are the things that attract those that don't know Him but want to know of His love. We are to be shining lights, living examples of what God has done for us. This also doesn't mean that we can't be successful and prosperous in this life either. It just means that we must possess the right spirit in all our workings. "But seek ye first the kingdom of God, and his righteousness; and all these things shall be added unto you" (Matt. 6:33). For us to exemplify our Creator, we must come to know our Creator. The more we seek earthly desires first, the further we separate ourselves from the source of our true happiness. If we are not operating with the assistance of the Holy Spirit, then we are under the influence of another spirit (see John 14:16–17).

Now is the time to break the curse of our ancestors. We may not possess their great power, but through the aid of the Holy Spirit, we can and will accomplish miraculous things. Now is the time for us to fulfill God's will, not our own, which is our true purpose for being here.

Chapter 5

Creating Habit

The Key to Preemptive Management

Finally, a new year is approaching! A very happy time indeed. Time for new beginnings, a time for new resolutions, and time for a brand-new me! This year is going to be the best year yet! I'm going to start eating right! I'm going to start exercising! I'm going to start saving money, and I am going to be more productive at work and toward accomplishing my dreams! As soon as January gets here, it is on! For right now, though, I'm going to kick back and enjoy this milkshake and fries, while I watch this new movie that just got released. Then I'm going to pass out all late so that I can sleep in tomorrow and be good and late and sluggish again for work tomorrow. *Hmm*! Sounds like a plan!

Is there anything that can be found wrong about this thought process as such? Or, how about this? Can there be anything right about it? The answer surprisingly is yes to both questions. The mere fact that this person is reciting the story of his/her future in their head in detail with passion and enthusiasm is absolutely the right thought process to have. Incidentally, the reciting of another story subsequently with the same passion and enthusiasm towards actions that may lead to a different not-so-fairytale ending always tends to create a tug-of-war of will in one's head. You see, to follow God's will there must be clarity of purpose. Without a defined direction, like this example of simple mental battles that we face 24/7, this tug-of-war is and always will be the mitigating factor that will lead us continually in the wrong direction if we are weak. We are the sum, the total of our daily habits. Habits are what make us strong because, once automated, these actions rarely require conscious thought. This leaves room or bandwidth, we could say, for us to envision new ideas and concepts. In other words: create!

Unlike our magnificent ancestors, we lack the mental capacity for remembering everything we see, touch, hear, or smell. Oh, and how this ability must have come in handy and aided them so well while they were fully engaged in planning an endeavor. The antediluvians were master planners and executers, but here is a thought: If this once extremely complex race used something so simple as the art of planning and strategizing precisely for grouping all minds on one accord before executing an endeavor, why is it that so many people in present day, who lack their physical and mental dexterity, so often skip this one simple step? Why is this art not used daily in accordance with our vision to accomplish everything that requires its use? Since we do not possess the full abilities of the first generations, wouldn't you think that we are most definitely in need of more plans indeed?

"It is a lack of moral courage—a will, strengthened and controlled by the spirit of God, to renounce hurtful habits" (White, *Testimonies for the Church*, vol. 5, p. 675).

The ability to create and maintain new habits that can completely alter the course of our lives for the better requires planning. "Good habits are hard to form and easy to live with. Bad habits are easy to form and hard to live with. Pay attention. Be aware. If we don't consciously form good ones, we will unconsciously form bad ones" (BukRate, https://1ref.us/1w8 [accessed April 4, 2022]).

We live in a society that for so long now have practiced indulgence—indulgence in everything the heart desires when it desires it (instant gratification). Once the remenance of these daily submissions to impulse have metastasized like a cancer, then and only then do most seek a remedy. Why is it that most people live out their lives constantly playing hurry-up defense? For isn't it a good offense that can predict what the other team is going to do simply by their formation and adapt accordingly? Isn't it a good offense that can score on the other team several times before the team even knows what hit them by using concise strategic actions continuously?

We must come to terms with and realize that it is of utmost importance, that if we intend to walk upright and live godly lives every day, the very foundation of this is in our daily habits. In the book *Christ's Object Lessons*, it states this:

> And let none flatter themselves that sins cherished for a time can easily be given up by and by. This is not so. Every sin cherished weakens the character and strengthens habit; and physical, mental, and moral depravity is the result. You may repent of the wrong you have done, and set your feet in right paths; but the mold of your mind and your familiarity with evil will make it difficult for you to distinguish between right and wrong. Through the wrong habits formed, Satan will assail you again and again. (White, *Christ's Object Lessons*, p. 281)

If we are not consciously developing our good daily habits each and every day, then we are continuously falling victim to Satan's snares. The ultimate goal of the evil one is to render us inactive. No one has to worry about someone that is on the sidelines. We must be in the game to win the game. Our daily habits are the vehicles that carry us from point A to point B. It's up to us to determine what point A and point B will be and then adjust our daily habits accordingly and get to work. Yes! It takes some work to create new habits. Old bad habits don't just disappear; they must be replaced with good habits. So, how do we create a new habit? In the next few pages, we are going to explore the process of creating a new habit, how to solidify that practice once initiated, what's going on in the mind that makes this possible, and how good habits can completely increase your daily performance and inevitably change your life for good.

Creating Habit

Creating good habits is the key to preemptive management. What is preemptive management? Well, to break this down to really grasp the concept, we must look at preempt. It means to take action in order to prevent an anticipated event or occurrence from happening. This is having a strong offense. When the government realizes a possible threat, they investigate. Once this situation is deemed a definite threat, the government launches a preemptive strike to prevent it from ever happening. Same should we be in our lives. By monitoring our lives and learning what possible threats are out there, we can at that time learn what habits need to be formed to launch our own preemptive strike. A strike against bad health, lack of productivity, obesity, unkindness, lack of creativity, monotony, unhappiness, and the list goes on. By changing our daily habits, we can learn to gain control over all of these areas of our life again, thus, becoming strong vessels that the Lord can use in a mighty way to complete His work. Our God is a God of order. We have the choice, rather, to grow each and every day or remain stationary, to strive to be Christlike—though that is a walk of consistent growth.

There are three major components in the creation of a habit. There is the cue, routine, and the reward. Many people have daily routines and, often enough, they don't realize what they are. We wake up every morning and for most of us it's cued by the unwanted sound of an alarm clock sounding off continuously. Likewise, if anyone is like the old me, I needed an hour's worth of alarms just to reach my target wake-up time. This starts each day off on a negative note which, in turn, initiates the first negative habit of your morning. If your cue is negatively sourced, then it will ultimately produce a negative routine. Routines such as smacking the snooze button about twenty times until you have reached maximum capacity for sleep time or forcing yourself to get up, only to zombie walk to the kitchen to literally blindly prepare your first cup of joe (coffee)—in both of these situations there is a reward. In the first, the reward is when your head hits that pillow again after trying to smash your alarm clock through your nightstand. The comfort that is felt is pure bliss when your head sinks into that pillow for just a little longer and your body re-snugs itself into the covers. In the other example, the reward is that first sip of coffee in the morning, and for all the coffee drinkers out there, you know exactly what I'm referring to. That moment is pure bliss. Do I have your attention yet? These routines are so small that most people don't even notice them for what they are, because they are so ingrained in their subconscious that they have become an automated piece of every morning. In each scenario, the body craves the rewards from each routine so much at this point that it literally initiates the routine without a conscious thought. Habits are so powerful!

Now, the offsetting of bad habits requires the replacing of them with good ones. They won't just disappear; the subconscious mind likes to retain its subjects. This victory is possible, though it will just take a little analyzing and focus to achieve. First you must recognize the bad routine for what it is. If the mind can't see it, then it will be hard for the mind to go to work to fix it. Secondly, you must figure out what the negative/positive cue is. Pick a day and really focus on the details of what is done during the time frame leading up to your departure for work or whatever time frame that contains the routine you are trying to change. Also begin to pay attention to your reactions to the routines so that you can narrow down the reward. Once these have been identified, then you can plan.

Let's take a simple look at the first example with the alarm clock and break it down. First! Why is the cue negative? Could it possibly be that you went to bed late the night before so you're tired and don't want to get out of bed? Or is it that you don't like your job—and maybe the people you work with—and dread each morning getting out of bed because you know that you will have to endure another day with them? Whatever it may be, you must pinpoint it. Realize this, whether it is a positive driving force or a negative one, because then you will know what tactic will be needed to condition a positive routine. For example, if your reason for the delayed exit from your bed each morning is the fact that you go to bed late every night, then your tactic would be to pick an earlier bedtime and begin to make a habit of that. By concentrating your beginning effort on this tactic, you will begin to incrementally convert your morning cue from a negative start to positive start. Also, one little tidbit that could also help tremendously with the creation of this new habit is gaining knowledge of our natural circadian rhythm. This internal clock alerts the body as to when it is time to sleep and wake—it is at its best with consistency. So, pick a bedtime and stick with it, and eventually you will be able to wake without even the use of an alarm clock.

Most of our days are simply filled with multiple cues that lead to routines that produce rewards, and some routines even become cues. Seems like an endless cycle of automated actions, doesn't it? So, why can't we control our lives? Learn to control the actions and you gain control over your life. Even in ancient times, there was sufficient knowledge of the great power of forming good habits. Aristotle once stated that "We are what we repeatedly do… therefore excellence is not an act but a habit" (Daily Stoic, https://1ref.us/1w9 [accessed April 4, 2022]). In 2 Peter, it explains how we are enslaved by what masters us.

"While they promise them liberty, they themselves are the servants of corruption: for of whom a man is overcome, of the same is he brought in bondage" (2 Peter 2:19). If we want to put up a better fight against the dark forces that want to keep us in bondage, we must concentrate our efforts on our daily routines.

The mind dislikes change very much. Our minds are actually hardwired to instinctively fear change. Why is that? Change itself, or even the thought of this mind-boggling experience, sends our primitive brain into absolute threat mode. The interesting thing, though, is that the associated mood change often goes unnoticed but continues to reoccur nonetheless. You see, most of our daily routines, as well as for most of our work habits, happen due to repetition over time, becoming habitual. Which means that these tasks, over time, require less and less conscious thought to execute. Often when this cycle is interrupted, our minds react and counter with resistance, but we don't consciously realize what is happening in the moment because it's an instinctual survival response.

The basal ganglia, as we learned in chapter 2, is responsible for the habitual behavior. The basal ganglia are, of course, the part of the brain that oversees habit learning. What is interesting, though, is how the sudden differing vibration of new stimuli stimulates the prefrontal cortex and causes such a negative reaction to change. This occurrence that initiates the resistance is what often deters people during their process—or could be process—of change

(Lumen, "Structure and Function of the Brain," https://1ref.us/1wn [accessed May 10, 2022]). The prefrontal cortex is linked directly to the amygdala, which is the most primitive part of the human brain. The amygdala, as we learned in chapter 2, is our natural security system and its functions are associated with our flight or fight response. So, when the prefrontal cortex is overloaded with new or unfamiliar information, the amygdala naturally goes into hyperdrive and creates this psychological imbalance, which can manifest itself as anxiety, fear, sadness, depression, anger, or fatigue, thus solving the grand mystery as to why change can be so hard. We are literally fighting against ourselves!

Are you beginning to grasp now as to why the formation of good habits to outweigh the bad is of such importance? Our conscious minds are battling against so much each day, and currently during this day and age, there are so many distractions that we can't even track them all. It must boil down to this simple fact: The more that we learn to automate our important routines, the better we will become, and with the betterment of ourselves, the more successful in all things we will be all the time—*the art of preemptive management.*

The art of habit forming is not the easy road to take, but neither is the Christian walk, is it? In life, we are constantly being positioned at the starting line, always facing two paths that lead to two very different races. On the left, you have the brisk walk marathon that is held indoors on a beautiful track in a nice temperature-controlled facility. On the right, you have the rocky cross-country mountain survival run where you face all the elements and possibly all the creatures as well. The danger level could quite possibly be astronomical. The results being: One leads you to a nice little ceremony where you stand on some blocks and get a metal placed around your neck and handed some flowers. A few cheers, a few snaps of the camera and it's done. On the other hand, the other leads you to total mind and body transformation and sets you up for a completely brand-new exciting life. No going back, the future is so bright now. Why? Well because you have faced all your fears during this race and have overcome them. You did things and reacted to situations in such a way that you never thought you possessed the aptitude to surmount. It is with that paradigm shift that your mind has finally discovered infinite possibilities that it couldn't see before. Unfortunately, though, if the race is never run or if we continue to stick to the indoor track because of conditioning, that door may never be opened for that beautiful rewarding light to shine in. Leap into your day's destiny purposefully by setting yourself up to win preemptively.

The key to successfully solidifying a new habit or new behavior lies in five actionable steps.

Step 1: Make the Unfamiliar, Familiar

Since the brain enjoys familiarity so much, give it what it needs to succeed. We learned about how much food can affect the brain's performance, and since we need all of our brain power to live awesome, productive days continually, one good habit would be to eat a wholesome breakfast every morning. One thing you can do to prep for the transformation of this daily routine would be to look up and print out tons of healthy breakfast ideas with pictures. Post these pictures everywhere you frequent in your home. Place on the bathroom mirror, refrigerator, car dash, desk at work (if able), and anywhere else you can think of. Begin to prepare and try these recipes and get family and friends in on it so that it can be fun. The result is the attaching of a positive emotion to the experience. Converting unfamiliar into familiar requires a bit of autosuggestion in the beginning stages, but the more stimuli that can be received through the five senses and be paired with a positive emotion, the faster the conversion process. When our minds begin to see the hard and the difficult as easy and fun and this becomes normalcy, imagine the power that we gain over ourselves at that very moment.

Step 2: Repetition

Repetition: the action of repeating something that has already been said or written. By making the unfamiliar familiar, you are defining what it is the mind is to focus on. The first step is crucial to your success, for it writes and speaks in favor of the new desired behavior. Creating the atmosphere where the mind can take in huge doses of examples and cues for the desired behavior through an array of sources by each of the five senses creates that significance in the mind to capture and hold that feeling. That feeling eventually becomes part of the cue by which the mind uses daily for the continuation of the daily action. The only way this all works is through repetition. Some say that to set a habit you must do it consecutively for thirty to sixty to even 120 days without missing more than a day in between. If you miss a day, it is OK; your success rate for setting that new behavior doesn't go down that drastically but to miss two days in a row, well this brings down your chances of successfully setting that new behavior very drastically.

The mind enjoys the familiar. So, to repeat a new, unfamiliar action daily, the body will most likely retaliate. Your mind will begin trying to negotiate its way out of any attempt for daily repetition. The success of this comes through determination stretched over time. You must consistently visualize your success even though you are failing miserably. Trust the beginning failure; it is part of the process. Most people never make it past this stage and that is why change is so hard for most individuals. Use cues to your advantage. Place in front of you that which you desire to do. You want to run every morning, place your running shoes and outfit beside your bed so that it is the first that you see in the morning. You want to eat breakfast every morning, prep the night before so that preparation is easy after a nice workout and shower. Become preemptive minded! Attack before bad health attacks you!

Step 3: Conscious, Quantitative Thought and Actions

While going through the beginning stages where failure is emanant, your focus must be on the failures but not in a negative sense. You must become your own personal Sherlock Holmes. In a way, this means becoming your own personal detective. Sherlock Holmes was known for his deductive reasoning skills, which he would use to narrow down the missing link to solve each crime. What most people don't know, though, is that it was the combination of deductive and inductive reasoning that made Sherlock Holmes so effective (Medium, "The Sherlock Holmes Conundrum," https://1ref.us/1wa [accessed April 4, 2022]). Deductive reasoning begins with an assumed first principle and you find logical conclusions from that. This method is usually used if there is no data to go on. Meaning you must think in theory to create your points of observation. Inductive reasoning is the development of generalizations from small systematic observations. Meaning that there is data already for you to compile your theories from. The key word in all of this is observation. What is preventing you daily from being successful in setting a new routine? What can be useful and aid in the setting of this new behavior that will eventually lead to a new you? Your days should be your own personal case study. That's how you begin to live on purpose. Becoming conscious of your existing daily routines and what the cues and rewards are for those gives you a road map, a blueprint, by which strategic planning can begin and actions can be implemented. By way of this newfound focus, your actions become measurable and your successes and areas that need improvement become visible.

Step 4: Positive Focus

For transformation to occur, there must be strong emotion wrapped around a positive thought. The first three steps will only begin to work successfully over time. So, you must remain in a positive state of mind to allow yourself to make the journey toward success. As we have learned, the mind enjoys regularity so, in the beginning, it will fight you to the very end. One of the most effective weapons in its arsenal is reoccurring negative thoughts. These thoughts stop progress in its track several times daily. To gain control of your daily mindset, you must nurture your mind each morning to give it strength to face the day. We should now understand the significance of the role that food has on the mind. We also should understand now the importance of altering our daily routines to ensure our success. Now understand that this is how it's all linked together. Start each day with a healthy breakfast or else the brain chemistry will be off and it will be harder for you to cultivate a positive mental attitude for the day. Read or listen to something positive each morning. You must put in what you want to come out. The more positive that you surround yourself with, the faster transformation can happen. In the Bible, it even states that "Finally, brethren, whatsoever things are true, whatsoever things are honest, whatsoever things are just, whatsoever things are pure, whatsoever things are lovely, whatsoever things are of good report; if there be any virtue, and if there be any praise, think on these things" (Phil. 4:8).

We are, and we become, what we think about. You can do what you say you can do! If you want to exercise daily, and you started the first day and felt like you were going to pass out, guess what your mind will tell you when it comes time for you to go back to the gym for day two? Your to-do list will enter your mind with all its deadlines; it will remind you of how tired you are because you just finished a ten-hour shift. It will also bring up fear remembering how you felt after your first workout. This is where having a positive focus comes to your aid. Instead of dwelling on the negative thoughts, because they will come—it's inevitable. You focus on the person you want to become and let that emotion encompass your entire being. That's what will push you when your mind says no.

Step 5: Prayer

"Those things, which ye have both learned, and received, and heard, and seen in me, do: and the God of peace shall be with you" (Phil. 4:9).

"I can do all things through Christ which strengtheneth me" (Phil. 4:13).

The journey towards new habit formation is anything but an easy ride, although I've learned along the way that it's the ride that really matters anyway. To live a purpose -illed life in representation of our Creator, there must be obstacles and there must be challenges. How else does His wonderous power shine bright through our lives if we are not seen as overcomers? By taking this journey of reconstructing our behaviors, we are showing our Creator that we wish to be aligned with His will. Our God is a God of order, and it is when we finally organize our daily routines to serve God in automation that we begin to see God fulfill things in our life that we never thought could be possible.

If we look at all those in the Bible that God considered to be perfect in His eyes, you notice a few similar characteristics shared by all of them.

1. They were in constant communion with God—Consistent
2. They prayed without ceasing—Loyal
3. They displayed a complete and utter dependence on God to accomplish anything—Humble
4. They possessed a very strong faith in God—Respectful
5. They all carried God's message throughout the land—Honor

These characteristics were formed through repetition of the actions associated with them. In other words, these were daily routines that were strengthened over time. You see, if we just move in faith, God will fill in the gaps where we lack and make us whole. Just take consistent action and He will point you in the right direction. "The LORD is nigh unto all them that call upon him, to all that call upon him in truth. He will fulfil the desire of them that fear him: he also will hear their cry, and will save them" (Ps. 145:18–19).

We can accomplish nothing on our own, but "with God all things are possible" (Matt. 19:26). We are all called to fulfill a great work. It's up to us as to how grand our part will play in this great work. God can use anyone in any condition to fulfill His work. The beauty of this whole thing is that He grants us the choice. We can choose how big our roles will be in the expansion of His kingdom. By structuring our lives to model after Jesus' life here on earth, we present to God an optimum vessel to be used by Him. "And when they had prayed, the place was shaken where they were assembled together; and they were all filled with the Holy Ghost, and they spake the word of God with boldness" (Acts 4:31).

We are the sum total of our daily habits. Our lives are shaped by the repeated actions that we consciously and unconsciously perform each day. If you want your life to change in any way, begin with your daily routines. It is said that it takes twenty-one days to form a new habit. The truth is that it can take anywhere from 60–120 days, in some cases longer than that, to solidify a new practice as a daily routine. One of the greatest habits that everyone could use is the daily showing of gratitude. What is gratitude? Well, it's thankfulness or gratefulness. It's a feeling of appreciation felt by and/or having a similar positive response shown by the recipient of kindness, gifts, help, favors, other types of generosity, towards the giver of such gifts. The formation of this very habit alone will help you begin to align yourself with God's will for your life. With each daily expression of gratitude, you begin to internalize more and more this concept of thankfulness for what our Creator has done and will always do for us in love! As we continue to develop this habit, we will begin to see our lives changing. Day by day we will notice that more and more our lives are resembling Christ. Our actions are becoming more Christlike, full of thankfulness, gratefulness, kindness, helpfulness, and love. So, today my challenge to you is to write down seven things that you are most thankful for. Each morning, as soon as you wake, drop to your knees and let this be your prayer to God. After each prayer reflect on these things you prayed for and as you do, you will soon notice a lot more that you have to be thankful for. What the mind doesn't see the heart doesn't feel! So, make your mind aware today.

"If my people, which are called by my name, shall humble themselves, and pray, and seek my face, and turn from their wicked ways; then will I hear from heaven, and will forgive their sin, and will heal their land" (2 Chron. 7:14).

Chapter 6

The Process

The Concepts of Change

To truly understand the concepts of change, one's perception of the subject in its entirety must be brought back into the confines of reality. Then and only then can the very essential belief factor, which is a catalyst for change, be cultivated and conveyed to aid an individual during a very possible transformation process.

Is change really possible? Can a person's behavioral patterns really be altered once they have been set? These have been heated topics of discussion in social circles around the world for many centuries. Many believe that once a _____ always a _____. This can be true, but there are always possibilities for exceptions, especially if you allow God to help. Change isn't easy; let's be clear about that. Particularly the process of change isn't easy at all. If the process is viewed, though, in comparison to the current behavioral persona a person possesses, along with its contributing factors multiplied over the number of years, months, days, and hours that it took to set those behaviors, then the process for change begins to lose a little of its intimidation—but not much. Most individuals' neuropathways are set by the age of twenty-five. By age thirty, it appears it would take a few sticks of dynamite, and maybe some composition C-4, to redirect the flow of ones' neuropathways by this time, but change is still possible. During these early years, it is very critical what one experiences during these times leading up to the big twenty-five. Think about it! If someone spends their early twenties working dead-end jobs with no real direction, partying a lot and using drugs recreationally, what are they really doing? Maybe they are conditioning their neuropathways to operate with no real direction, no discipline, and to consistently rely on the stimulation of drugs, alcohol, and other sources just for the body to produce any kind of dopamine response so that they may feel something (good) or be happy. On the other hand, many youngsters are in college during these years. Those experiences in themselves could be extremely beneficial or extremely impede someone from the proper development of future healthy neuropathways. If one is overstressed, secluded, highly overworked without any time for self, and a people pleaser for all four to eight years in college, a host of behavioral patterns are being formed that will shape that persons' future neuro habit loop. One could condition their neuropathways to not operate energetically unless in high stress environments (i.e., high-paying eighty- to ninety-hour-a-week jobs). One could develop an inability to make the proper neuro connections necessary for the formation of real bonding relationships and end up a hermit well into their thirties and beyond. One could also end up lacking the ability to have fun and to entertain themselves, much less anyone else. One could stretch themselves to thin consistently with the inability to say no because they want to cater to everyone but themselves. These patterns tend to shape our characters for the future. We wonder why we keep doing the same things over and over again, ofttimes expecting different results. We do it because it's been hardwired into our brains, the handiwork of our environments.

These modern-day so-called gurus are always saying, "You wanna [and yes, I said wanna] change your life? Change your mind." What does that mean exactly? It's not like you can swap out your brain for a new one. This isn't an auto shop where you can just swap out an engine when the old one seizes up. I always like to say, "Change your habits, change your thoughts, change your actions, and you change your life." All this is true, but how? They have their ways of going about it but ofttimes God is not at the center of it, and yes, I am referring to the uppercase G God!

"But Jesus beheld them, and said unto them, With men this is impossible; but with God all things are possible" (Matt. 19:26).

"For with God nothing shall be impossible" (Luke 1:37).

Where to Start?

This all must begin with the willingness to change, because if the mind doesn't realize the necessity for change, the body will not follow. All good things begin and end well with prayer. So, that must be a good place to start! Start praying to God for the changes you want to occur in your life. At the beginning of the process, you must recognize that you can't and will not be able to do this on your own.

"O Lord my God, I cried unto thee, and thou hast healed me" (Ps. 30:2).

What is prayer, really? Prayer—the true definition of prayer—is a relationship. The importance and the power of prayer is often overlooked because people neglect to really take the time to understand what prayer truly is. It's how we humbly worship, communicate, and sincerely seek some real face time with our Creator. Through prayer, we show our complete and utter dependence upon God for everything. Our attitudes toward this sacred action must be ones of humbleness not haughtiness. We must always seek prayer before all else, because praying continually is how we keep our link to the Source of all power. God is omnipotent and omnipresent, meaning He is all powerful and present everywhere at the same time. Prayers must come often and regularly, not as if we are obligated but from a humble heart. Our prayers should be like we are talking to our best friend, with compassion and love, curiosity, and empathy. Prayer is for our benefit, not God's, for it is through prayer that we our brought up to God, not the other way around. We must be brought to God through Jesus Christ by way of the Holy Spirit through prayer. Oh, how our lives will begin to change once we grasp this simple fact.

With prayer, the direction of our lives will begin to move in the right direction. We must keep in mind always though the mindset (attitude) in which we must carry toward prayer to be humble, patient, and open minded. God's answer to our prayers won't always come the way we expect. We must be ready to accept that God knows best! If we could see through some all-knowing, infinite spectacles and be able to see the big picture, then we would understand how God works, but we can't. That's why it requires FAITH.

"For my thoughts are not your thoughts, neither are your ways my ways, saith the LORD. For as the heavens are higher than the earth, so are my ways higher than your ways, and my thoughts than your thoughts" (Isa. 55:8–9).

We must truly trust God and His process for any of this to really have a huge impact on our lives. Ofttimes, it is we ourselves that prevent God from fulfilling His will for us.

In the electric wiring of an automobile, problems tend to occur that prevent components from operating correctly or at all. These problems can usually always be linked to at least one of the six usual culprits for electrical issues in an automobile. These occurrences prevent continuity. Now, what continuity is, is the unbroken and consistent existence or operation of something over a period of time. These six common electrical problems are as such:

1. Corrosion
2. Water Damage
3. Loose Connection
4. Fried Wire—Short
5. Load Damage
6. Source of Power Depleted

With corrosion there is usually some sort of build-up on the wire(s) or metal contact surface, preventing the continual flow of power through the circuit. Water damage causes rusting, which is a form of corrosion; it also can cause shorts by causing power surges in a circuit, frying wires. A loose connection is an improper connection between metal contact surfaces, preventing sufficient current flow. Of course, shorts are when something causes excessive amounts of current to flow through a circuit that is not strong enough to handle the power flow, so it fries. A load is the object in the circuit that is set to do work. So, for instance, a light bulb is the load in a light circuit and its work is to produce light by absorbing the current flow and converting it. Finally, last but not least, is the depleted power source. The power source is usually the battery or whatever is used to store the energy. All of these issues are repairable. They are not always easy to repair but they are repairable, nonetheless.

We must remain hardwired to our source of power to remain strong and courageous through any transformation process. Just like with the electrical problems, we are all often faced with these same symptoms. These issues, in turn, block or restrict our continuity of power from our Creator. It is our job to be ever watchful and recognize these symptoms so that we may repair them. We are to become our own personal mechanics, for it is by choice that we allow God's power to move in us. By the choices we make daily, we choose to remove the corrosion, the water damage. We choose to tighten the connection, to increase the gauge of wire so that when the power comes, our circuits can handle the power. We change out our light bulbs when they are inoperable so that God isn't blocked from doing work in us. We have more control over our lives than we think. The best thing about it all is that our power source, which is God, is never depleted. We are usually just faced with the symptoms that end up hindering, obscuring, and sedating God's enormous power from us. Symptoms that are caused by our choices and our environments.

"Study to shew thyself approved unto God, a workman that needeth not to be ashamed, rightly dividing the word of truth" (2 Tim. 2:15).

One of the most important pieces in the transformation process is the learning of how to hear God's voice when He speaks to us. Through every journey, the trip is a lot smoother with a knowledgeable guide. But how do we hear His voice? More importantly, how do we know when it is, in fact, God that is trying to speak with us? Well for starters, if you are trying to establish a relationship with someone, you begin with a conversation, right? Going back to why beginning with prayer is so important and ultimately leads to understanding the all-encompassing meaning of the action, which is to begin the dialog that will lead to a meaningful relationship. What are you really seeking? To really have a great relationship with someone, you must get to know them on a multitude of levels. How else can you know what to expect from them or how to better coexist with them? Please tell me, how can you learn how to maneuver with them, around them (in their presence), and for them? This social progression only takes place over time, quality time, spent with the individual(s). Learning about them, their loves, hates, fears, goals, mannerisms, characteristics, and likes. So, how do you plan on getting to know God better since He is not physically embodied here with us? How do we get to know Him so that we may share this type of relationship with Him? Through study! By the reading and applying of God's Word (the Bible), we open the door of communication with God. He begins to speak to us through His Word. As He reveals Himself to us continually during our time spent studying His character, His likes, His dislikes, His goals, visions, and loves are revealed to us and our relationship with Him grows stronger and stronger. Then and only then we begin to know what to expect from Him, we begin to understand how He works, and what it looks like when He is working. We learn of how He loves, and what His perfect vision and plans are for us. These eye-opening revelations are a must-have during any transformation process that warrants new success. By discovering who God is, we can then discover who we are to be.

"Again I say unto you, That if two of you shall agree on earth as touching any thing that they shall ask, it shall be done for them of my Father which is in heaven. For where two or three are gathered together in my name, there am I in the midst of them" (Matt. 18:19–20).

Last, but most definitely not the least, is our associations. By studying, you gain a model of what being Christlike is all about, of which there is no substitute. However, going through this journey alone is not the answer. It is made very clear in Matthew 18:19–20 that we are to come together with likeminded individuals in prayer and in study. How else are we to learn how to agree with each other? Through this process, a bond and strengths are formed, because others' strengths may be your weaknesses and vice versa. The sharing of information relevant to the assistance of your newfound goals in Christ is of utmost importance. Learning from these individuals that have been walking the path a little longer, helps to navigate a straighter path for you. The knowledge that is gained here, through this union, is of such a value that there is no equal by far. Also, through this congregation of likeminded individuals, a platform is being laid out for the ushering in of the Holy Spirit. The Holy Spirit is God's power in motion. God sends out His Spirit through a projection of energy to any location to accomplish His will, His eyes ofttimes sighted in on those that prove themselves to be ready to receive Him. On the day of Pentecost, the disciples received the Holy Spirit on this earth for the first time in history (Acts 2:4). The one underlying characteristic that is still as relevant today as it was on that day so many years ago, is simply this!

"And when the day of Pentecost was fully come, they were all with one accord in one place" (Acts 2:1).

Now what does it really mean to be in one accord? It means that they do something together or at the same time, because they simply agree about what should or needs to be done. When people that are likeminded can come together and are as one (in agreement), there is POWER in their midst—God's power.

"Can two [truly] walk together, except they be agreed?" (Amos 3:3)

There are a few guidelines that can be followed when choosing those to associate with. These can be considered tells that can be looked for and, therefore, in some cases, instantly know if the individuals in consideration will have your and their best interest at heart. For one, what is the atmosphere like when these individuals are together? The Lord has blessed us with a pretty good sensory perception that can signal us as to the quality of an environment if we pay attention to it. Is the atmosphere spiritual? Does it exemplify the fruits of the spirit which are love, joy, peace, longsuffering, gentleness, goodness, faith, meekness, and temperance (Gal. 5:22–23)? You can really sense if someone is truly walking the path of a Christian by witnessing their daily lives. Are they living, or attempting to live out, what they believe or are they simply going through the motions? Now, I'm not saying that all these things have to be lined up for you to make a decision, because let's face it, we will not find a perfect environment here on earth. With that being said though, there are environments that could quite possibly be more perfect or more suitable for a person depending upon their developmental needs, social needs, need for bare necessities, and/or structural necessities at any appointed time. All these possibilities should be taken into thorough consideration when contemplating who to surround yourself with.

"[E]very good tree bringeth forth good fruit; but a corrupt tree bringeth forth evil fruit" (Matt. 7:17).

As we go through this journey, God begins to speak with us. We begin to notice the voice of the Holy Spirit. Some people refer to this voice as instinct or as an innate self-preservation mechanism initiated by our natural flight or fight response. I say from experience it is our natural link to infinite intelligence and the way we access this fully is by keeping ourselves in tuned with our Creator. My Mom used to always tell me, "You know how to tell if it is God's voice that is speaking to you?"

Me: "How?"

Mom: Well, there are three things to keep in mind while contemplating rather the voice is from God or just your imagination or outside influences. If you feel that God is speaking to you, especially about making an important decision, ask yourself these three questions:

1. Is whatever it is in line with His Word (the Bible)?
2. Is He opening whatever doors that are required to be opened?
3. Do you feel at peace with whatever it may be?

If you can answer yes to all three of these questions, then feel confident that God is taking the lead and you are on the right path still."

To the Churches:

We must understand that change does not happen overnight. It is a process that we all must go through in order to become better, more aware people. Once we understand the process, the learning curve is then shortened because we don't get set back as far when negative occurrences arise.

The Process

One of the most important entities one needs when going through the process of change is the church. When God begins to work on someone, they begin to feel uncomfortable in their environment. Stimuli that used to excite them to the core doesn't feel so special anymore; something is missing. What is missing? This is when the search begins. From one place to the next in the current environment all corners are checked, all rocks flipped over. What can fill this huge void? This is God working. Then finally, through whatever source God chooses to use, they find their way to a church.

Saints need to understand that this is the most critical time in a new believer's—or believers gone astray—journey. After all of this searching, they finally find a new environment. The environment they have been hoping for and unconsciously praying for. Now, once they find this new environment, one full of support, love, people that can be trusted, people who care, people teaching and living a better way—is this what they truly find? Or do they come upon a place where no one appears to be happy, no one is prosperous, everyone is gossiping, everyone is in a clique, everyone is arguing over politics or Scriptures as if they are having a dance off trying to prove who is the better "CHRISTIAN"?!

We must understand that for someone possibly with zero to no belief in anything, that they may be fragile. Life may have beaten them as water beats the rocks on the shore. Once they have finally come upon the grounds of the church and work up enough courage to walk through that door, they must instantly find themselves engulfed in God's presence, even if they don't understand what that means quite yet. The presence should be undeniable and felt to the core. We are the representatives of Christ and are specifically instructed on the necessities by which our vessels may be continually used to do God's work.

> The servants of Christ are not to act out the dictates of the natural heart. They need to have close communion with God, lest, under provocation, self rise up, and they pour forth a torrent of words that are unbefitting, that are not as dew or the still showers that refresh the withering plants. This is what

Satan wants them to do; for these are his methods. It is the dragon that is wroth; it is the spirit of Satan that is revealed in anger and accusing. But God's servants are to be representatives of Him. He desires them to deal only in the currency of heaven, the truth that bears His own image and superscription. The power by which they are to overcome evil is the power of Christ. The glory of Christ is their strength. They are to fix their eyes upon His loveliness. Then they can present the gospel with divine tact and gentleness. And the spirit that is kept gentle under provocation will speak more effectively in favor of the truth than will any argument, however forcible. (White, *The Desire of Ages*, p. 353)

Chapter 7

The Process Continued

Change Is Possible. Believe

I grew up in the church. I was lucky to have a mother that decided to change her life by giving it to God while she was pregnant with me. She tried her very best to create for me a firm foundation in the Lord. I remember sitting in church during the week, bored at a very young age, and with me that only led to mischief. My mother was very active in church; we were either at prayer meeting or choir rehearsal it seemed like always. I didn't understand it then, the influx of activities that we were constantly engaged in, but I see now that they were teaching us. They were teaching us how to construct new, exceptionally beneficial habits. Habits that would lead us towards Christ instead of away from Him. This was the true definition of church and church family. We were always at one another's houses and not just on the weekend but any day of the week. We knew each other well outside of church. We went camping in the mountains together, had fruit sales and Christmas tree sales together. We would go horseback riding, go on hay rides, bonfires, and picnics. We had a softball team and basketball team that played quite often. We as kids played kick the can and kickball in the church school parking lot. It was, I have to admit, some of the best times of my life. As the years went by, people moved, things changed, and I grew up. As some do, when I grew up, I drifted away from the church, and when I use the term "drift," I really mean sped off in a high-powered speed boat completely in the wrong direction. To me it didn't have the same feel as before, and by this time, I had found something a little more alluring. I never turned off my belief in God during these times. I just wasn't expressing much love for Him. My love was directed towards the world and its many splendors. In all my ignorance, all of my good habits that were established over these years slowly turned bad. One by one it seemed as if my good habits were being replaced with new ones until one day, I took notice and saw that I was standing in complete darkness. To be in this world without God at your side can be a very dangerous place.

I found myself spending all of my time in all the wrong places. First came smoking cigarettes. I used to play around like I was smoking in the beginning just to fit in. I wouldn't inhale, I would just puff and blow the smoke out to look cool. Once I started that, though, I had to keep the lie going at that point, so I got good at being convincing. I taught myself how to blow out smoke rings and how to blow smoke out through my nose, still with no inhaling, but I looked like a pro so to everyone else I had to be inhaling! Amazing the lengths that young people will go to just to impress some knuckleheads. You see, the devil doesn't just come up on you like a cat pouncing on a mouse. It's not always that recognizable. Never that easy. He's too clever for that. He slowly primes you, getting you ready for what he has planned for you. One step after another, one cookie or dollar bill after another, he methodically leads you away from your Creator.

Before I knew it, I was smoking cigarettes like a boss. The only difference now, I was inhaling but not only that, it was a-pack-a-day habit. I always smelled like stale cigarettes, and you don't really grasp the true stench of that habit until you finally quit and get the luxury of smelling someone else that smokes, ugh! I was a slave to that habit, always having to go outside in whatever weather conditions just to feed the craving. If I ran out, I would literally go crazy and end up driving insane distances in the middle of the night sometimes just for a cigarette. When the devil puts something on you, he uses vices that will control how you spend your time. The ultimate goal is to keep you distracted, leading you further and further away from the light. Smoking was my gateway. As soon as I was comfortable with that, I moved on to guns, drugs, alcohol, and girls—and that's not to say that guns are bad! It's what you do with the guns that determines your moral aptitude. Once the devil has led you away and captured your attention, that's when he hits you hard.

What We Are Up Against

The gateway to our inner worlds (the mind) is through our senses. The five senses are our sense of sight, sense of taste, sense of sound, sense of smell, and sense of touch. These are considered the traditionally recognized methods of perception. Now, if perception is the way of regarding, understanding, and/or interpreting something, what would it truly gain someone to have complete control over all the avenues (receptors) that lead to your clarity? Bear with me now, there's a point. Clarity is the quality of being clear or, in particular, it's also the quality of coherence and intelligibility. All relative to perception! Can someone really grab ahold and steer another's human experience through these senses?

> Satan's Strategy Is to Confuse the Senses—Satan's work is to lead men to ignore God, to so engross and absorb the mind that God will not be in their thoughts. The education they have received has been of a character to confuse the mind and eclipse the true light. Satan does not wish the people to have a knowledge of God; and if he can set in operation games and theatrical performances that will so confuse the senses of the young that human beings will perish in darkness while light shines all about them, he is well pleased. (White, *The Adventist Home*, p. 401)

Our realities are formed through our perceptions. These perceptions are shaped using stimuli that are received through our senses. As the mind receives this sensory information, it processes it and responds accordingly by using past experiences as a reference point in finding an appropriate action or response to the perceived meaning of the stimuli. In other words, the brain is in a constant state of redefining normality based solely on surrounding stimuli. Too much garbage in, garbage begins to be expected in the outward. Hence the importance of maintaining the control of the number of positive stimuli consistently coming in. Ever heard the statement "guilty by association" or "show me where and who you spend the bulk of your time with and I'll show you your future"? We are all electrically charged. It flows all around us, through us, and even through the air. This power, this power that connects us all, is inescapable. If you know anything about how electricity works, you know that there is a positive and a negative charge. If you understand how atoms are formed, which is the base of all matter, there it is again, a positive proton and a negative electron. We have to face this fact no matter where we go, but the one thing we can decide is which side we will dwell in predominantly. It is because we are all connected that we must be careful. If a negative environment with very negative people is frequented and your mind isn't conditioned strongly enough to the positive side to resist the negative, eventually your mind and body will begin to harmonize with the charge that is present. Our bodies respond to outside stimuli with emotion. Emotion, strongly concentrated, creates in us such a powerful charge of energy that it not only affects our entire bodies but also sends out that charge to anyone that is around us. Emotions are the adjoining pathways from our minds to our bodies.

"Energy is not lost or destroyed, it is merely transferred from one party to the next." –Sir Isaac Newton (The Book of Threes, https://1ref.us/1wb [accessed April 11, 2022]).

It is so important which charge we choose to dominate the world around us. Yes, we have a choice! If we are constantly allowing our emotions to be manipulated to lean towards the negative charge, it is our fault. Even with the unavoidable negative stimuli that will inevitably creep in at times, that can be contained! We have the power to choose how our minds process this undesired content. If the mind has been conditioned to see the bright side of things always, the mind will find a positive way to process the unwanted stimuli. If the mind has been conditioned to link the new stimuli to a negative past experience, though, then, well, you know. Repetition (of thought) is conditioning, looping back to why forming good habits (thought habits) is so beneficial. It's hard to create new, good habits, especially if you have none and are not around anyone else that's trying to do the same also. That's why like-minded individuals gravitate toward like-minded individuals; it's because they are on the same charge, wavelength, path, whatever you want to call it. If you find yourself in an environment and there is something that always nags at you and makes you feel uneasy even to the point where you can't even enjoy yourself anymore, this might be why, and God is maybe pushing you towards a different charge. Get around those that are functioning on the level that you want to be on. Yes, it will make you nervous (i.e., being around students, being around church folk, being around wholesome business men/women, being around entrepreneurs, and the list goes on). That's what it's supposed to feel like at first. Remember what the mind does with new information? It fights it. Why? The mind is always in search of normalcy, that's why getting outside of your comfort zone often is so important. It forces the mind to grow and eventually embrace a new, improved state of normalcy. Always challenge the norm!

The Impact That Society Has on the Senses

There are several ways in which our senses are manipulated routinely through our socio-economic driven world. If there were ever a question as to whether or not mind control exists and/or has anything to do with a persons' inability to change, walk with me for a moment! What I am about to share with you just might severely affect your present reality or state of normalcy. So, prepare for your mind to fight back. Or deep down you've already felt it and just couldn't put a finger on it and didn't know what it was, or you've known all along. Either way, it's important to see things as they really are and not as the productions that have been put in place for centuries.

There are so many areas that could be discussed that would highlight the many nuances that are associated with this subject. But for the sake of time and space, we are only going to dive into four categories. These four categories are the platforms that drive the most successful results in the art of corrupting.

The Entertainment Industry

Nowadays everyone wants to be a star! The insatiable hunger for fame and fortune is in some cases all-encompassing to the most passionate. The things people are willing to do, the things people are willing to give up is astonishing, just for the feeling of being idolized and coveted. The entertainment industry is full of these so-called stars, and people literally do worship them. The devil is very cunning and knows very well the power that these individuals possess. He knows how to package up and market sin to every demographic. He has had the lifetime of this earth to perfect his craft, and if we refuse to become diligent students of the Word and are not arming ourselves with the right tools to be able to spot the devils' work when it is right in our faces, then we will continue to be fooled and bamboozled every time.

One subject we must acquaint ourselves with is symbolism. It is through this that a whole host of messages containing a belief system is transferred right in front of our eyes daily. But most of us can't see them because our minds are not trained to spot them. For instance, what is a star? Most know a star as being a natural luminous body that is visible in the sky or an outstandingly talented performer in whatever field it may be, most commonly associated with the entertainment industry. Let's dive a little deeper—symbolism remember! For centuries, stars have been studied very closely by many cultures. This practice dates all the way back to the Egyptians and probably even predates them. Astrology has been a way of discovery and has produced several of our modern-day tools that we use every day without thought of where or why it came into existence. Star gazing has been a part of religious practices and also used for celestial navigation and orientation. The belief among different cultures has been that the stars are affixed to a heavenly sphere. This makes them immutable, therefore enabling them to be used as tracking devices that can pinpoint the position of other planets as well as the inferred position of the sun. Of course, tracking the suns movements became a necessity the moment we as a human race had to produce our own agriculture (result of sin in Eden). The process was accomplished by monitoring and logging the sun's motion against the background stars. This is how our modern-day Gregorian calendar that we all use every day was created (ThoughtCo, "Gregorian Calendar," https://1ref.us/1wc [accessed April 12, 2022]).

Now, here is the point, for centuries stars have carried and transferred a host of information to us. I mean, the elemental makeup of planets can even be determined through spectral lines which is the recording of light transferred from stars through a small opening and compared with the different signatures that each element emits (Astronomy, "How Do Scientists Determine the Chemical Compositions of the Planets and Stars?" https://1ref.us/1wd [accessed April 11, 2022]). This is why one of the old meanings of the word star is messenger, as the Babylonians believed the gods used stars to communicate with them (Librarypoint, "Early Astronomers," https://1ref.us/1ww [accessed May 10, 2022]). Is it possible that this is why stars in the entertainment industry are labeled as such? Their sole purpose is to be message-bearers! To carry out a message to the world that is everything but the message of God. Why are they used? Well, because they are visible to everyone; they have become familiar faces, therefore they influence heavily. Also look at the word *asterisk*, which contains *aster*, the Greek word for star (Dictionary, "Asterisk," https://1ref.us/1we [accessed April 11, 2022]). An asterisk is a figure of a star that is used in printing and writing as a reference to a passage or a note in the margin or to fill the space where words are omitted. These two uses are key, especially since every production in the entertainment industry starts on paper. A script is created for all theatrical performances and a song is written line by line in words and notes before it is ever recorded or performed. Entertainment is simply live motion depicting written stories or beliefs (messages). An asterisk is used as a reference to a passage or keynote, or to fill the space where words are omitted (left out or excluded).

If a company wants you to buy their product, they use a star in their commercials. If there is a new trend that someone wants to infect a generation with, they use stars to get it out to the people. In movies, where all sorts of evil doings are portrayed as good and cool, who are the stars that are used to play these leading roles? In the music industry, who are the stars used to depict materialism, gang violence, covetousness, sex, drugs, rebellion, spiritualism, and the love of money as normal good every day American values? When God is being omitted from our homes, our schools, our government, what do you think is the cause and what do you see being put in place of God? If you don't believe me, look for the patterns yourself. See if there is something that connects them all and shows that they bear the same message.

Symbolism is one thing that connects them all and is a powerful tool that is often used to show meanings, affiliations, qualities, and beliefs in plain sight only to be recognized by those that are in the know. If you don't understand what to look for, several images can be paraded right in front of you, with you none the wiser. Stars are considered artists and they learn to perfect this art—the use of symbolism. Symbolism is an artistic and poetic movement or style using symbolic images and indirect suggestion to express mystical ideas, emotions, and states of mind. Symbolism originated in late nineteenth century France and Belgium, spearheaded by important figures such as Mallarmé, Maeterlinck, Verlaine, Rimbaud, and Redon (Wikipedia, "Symbolism," https://1ref.us/1wf [accessed April 11, 2022]). Be very careful not to underestimate the power of this. For example, let's look at indirect suggestion. What is it? Indirect suggestions are considered suggestions that can circumvent the censorship of consciousness to reach the "unconscious" where they can activate dormant potentials. In other words, a form of hypnosis! Hypnosis is "a state of abnormal suggestibility and responsiveness, but decreased general awareness often brought about by concentration on a repetitive stimulus" (The Free Dictionary, "Hypnosis," https://1ref.us/1wg [accessed April 11, 2022]). Now, with all this being said, let's put it all together. All shows, movies, music, social media, and news that is intent on suggesting one state of mind, which is anything but having the mind of Christ, follows a certain format. This format is loaded with direct and indirect suggestions to cut right through our conscious mind straight to our subconscious or unconscious mind. This causes us to think, believe, feel, react, and act in certain ways and we don't even know why we do or feel these things.

"Be sober, be vigilant; because your adversary the devil, as a roaring lion, walketh about, seeking whom he may devour" (1 Peter 5:8).

These devices are meant to distract, misdirect, and desensitize the mind. To bring the human mind into harmony with the ultimate plan of the evil one (the complete removal of the one true God). If you doubt this, wake up and begin to watch with new eyes. All who are allied and aligned with the devil and his plan use symbolic languages to show their allegiance. There are so many, too many to list. My intent here is to simply spark an interest in those that are unaware so that they may begin to seek understanding.

"My people are destroyed for lack of knowledge: because thou hast rejected knowledge, I will also reject thee, that thou shalt be no priest to me: seeing thou hast forgotten the law of thy God, I will also forget thy children" (Hosea 4:6).

The major symbols used are the Baphomet, inverted pentagram, the covering of one eye (eye of Horace), the butterfly (representing a transformation), the black and white checker board, the A-OK symbol but with the fingers forming 666, the devil horns (made famous in rock music), the pyramid made with the hand gesture (made famous by a certain rapper), angel wings (representing the fallen angels), the serpent, the ankh, the obelisk (represents sun worship), the solar wheel (sun worship). These symbols mentioned are only a few. Begin to learn these and what they mean and then go back and watch and listen to our forms of entertainment and then you will begin to realize how it is all connected. You will also be astonished once you realize how far it goes back and how long we have unknowingly been rapaciously exposed to these ideologies.

With today's technology, we are consistently bulldozed each day with suggestions. The distractions and misdirecting are too numerous to count. How in this day and age are we to combat such inundation? Well, there are four areas in which energy should be directed towards the learning and mastering of. All the strategies in this whole book can be placed in one or more of these four categories.

Understanding

There are two parts to this word: the first is the ability to understand or comprehend something, the other is to be sympathetically aware of other peoples' feelings, also tolerant and forgiving. For the sake of understanding this chapter better, we will focus on the comprehension part. We must understand a few of the ways this modern world creates strongholds in all of us with the use of distraction and misdirection. Think about all the modern things that we have now at our disposal for a moment. Think about how easy it is to get sucked into or caught up in the many luxuries that we experience now. I'm not saying that all modern advances are bad by no means. This is just a little exercise to get you to realize the big picture. Think about what happens when you sit on the sofa and open your phone just to look at one thing that popped up on a social media platform. How much time passes before you actually get off your phone? Have you ever timed yourself?

> **Distraction:** "[A] thing that prevents someone from giving [their] full attention to something else. An extreme agitation of the mind or emotions" (Google, "Distraction," [accessed April 11, 2022]).
>
> Democrat versus Republican, racial injustices on the tube, celebrity drama, video after video showcasing anything that will capture and divert full attention, gender confusion, all negative current events.
>
> Distraction is something that makes it difficult to think or pay attention, something that amuses or entertains you so that you do not think about problems, work, world issues, life, etc.
>
> **Misdirection:** "The action or process of directing someone to the wrong place or in the wrong direction" (Lexico, https://1ref.us/1wh [accessed April 11, 2022]).

All of the symbology and subliminal messages used in Hollywood and the music industry direct people subtly and boldly away from

God and godly things. Politicians using these tactics divert attention away from the real bad news or new laws being slid into place, targeting our rights and our way of life. One thing being paraded in front of us to excite and hypnotize while the agenda is being slid in front of us in between the lines (lies).

"In theatrical magic, misdirection is a form of deception in which the performer draws audience attention to one thing to distract it from another. Managing audience attention is the aim of all theater, and the foremost requirement of all magic acts" (Wikipedia, "Misdirection (magic)." https://1ref.us/1wi [accessed April 11, 2022]).

Think about our society as it is today and tell me that most are not impacted by some form of distraction or misdirection. Our very society is designed to keep us distracted. They have to work to maintain all of the stuff and get more stuff and, if you have the luxury of living next to the Jones, well! Especially the ones that are fully sold out to this ideology and only come around to talk about or show off the new toy. People are stressing themselves out and making themselves sick, depressed, envious, jealous, hateful, and then they begin sowing seeds of discord just to make themselves feel better. People are driving themselves crazy trying to keep up and for what?

"Let your conversation be without covetousness; and be content with such things as ye have: for he hath said, I will never leave thee, nor forsake thee" (Heb. 13:5).

It was never God's plan for us to be just seekers of possessions and pleasure but to be hearers and doers of the Word so that His name may be glorified through us.

Our pleasure should be in the Lord. This brings us to the other condition that plagues our current generations. The devil is very cunning in his attack. Many of us suffer from cases of Anhedonia. Whether it be mild to severe or somewhere in between, it prevents us from drawing closer to God. How you say? This is how!

Anhedonia, or Anhedonic state, means without pleasure. Anhedonia occurs when there is a breakdown in the brains reward system. Every time someone feels pleasure the neurotransmitter chemical called dopamine fills the part of the brain called striatum (National Library of Medicine, "Dopamine Is Released," https://1ref.us/1wj [accessed April 11, 2022]). Anhedonia does its damage or causes its effects through the prefrontal cortex which regulates the release of the dopamine. The TV, smartphones, computers, and video games—all these devices while engaged in them—cause the mind to slip into a hypnotic state. Easier access to the subconscious mind is created, which is where strongholds in our minds are stored. The hypnosis is caused by the screen flicker, and it lowers our brain waves to an alpha state which can be associated with a state of meditation. Dopamine and other feel-good chemicals are also released during this time, which aids in causing the addiction. While in this state, the information viewed can be dropped right into the subconscious mind, altering current beliefs and forming new ones. It shifts your brain from operating out of the left side (critical analysis, logical thought) to the right side which tends to drop the ball on critically analyzing incoming data. It also happens to be where the prefrontal lobes are. Anhedonia is caused when there is a lower activity level in the prefrontal cortex. The prefrontal cortex is also responsible for our memory as well as helping us think more clearly. You see, the constant stream of high dopamine releasing entertainment has conditioned our minds to not accept any other forms of pleasure to be desirable. We are simply overstimulated! Have you noticed how it's getting harder and harder to get kids to go outside and play or to focus on anything outside of a device for more than an hour at a time? They are having issues with using their imaginations to play and entertain themselves like past generations did. With this comes impatience and has created the age of instant gratification which is a direct conflict with God's process of developing a relationship with Him. The Bible is to be dissected and learned line by line here a little and there a little (Isa. 28:13). We are to take pleasure in the process of getting to know our Creator. The Christian walk is a lifelong journey. The modern mindset is being conditioned away from this. Please tell me how we are to truly come to know our Creator if we are not putting in the time because we can't focus on the right things anymore. Way too many distractions!

In any challenge in life, there must be time taken to understand the roadblocks, the hurdles, the deterrents, the obstacles, oftentimes it doesn't happen overnight either. If there is no understanding, there is no recognized starting point for changing current behaviors to be in God's favor!

Prayer and Devotion

> No one but yourself can control your thoughts. In the struggle to reach the highest standard, success or failure will depend much upon the character, and the manner in which the thoughts are disciplined. If the thoughts are well girded, as God directs they shall be each day, they will be upon those subjects that will help us to greater devotion. If the thoughts are right, then as a result the words will be right; the actions will be of that character to bring gladness and comfort and rest to souls. (White, *Our High Calling*, p. 112)

Devotion – the root word is *devote,* meaning to commit by solemn act (Merriam-Webster, https://1ref.us/1wk [accessed April 11, 2022]). Devotion has to do with our worship, for without it, it is harder for God to instruct us. God is needed at the center whenever change in the right direction is trying to be accomplished. Devotion is the state of mind needed, the very frame of mind found in those humbly devoted to God. It is the spirit of complete awe, of reverence, and of respectful fear of our divine Creator. Devotion is intimately as well as divinely connected with prayer. The two are rarely separated.

> Prayer promotes the spirit of devotion, while devotion is favorable to the best praying. Devotion furthers prayer and helps to drive prayer home to the object which it seeks. Prayer thrives in the atmosphere of true devotion. It is easy to pray when in the spirit of devotion. The attitude of mind and the state of heart implied in devotion make prayer effectual in reaching the throne of grace. God dwells where the spirit of devotion resides. All the graces of the Spirit are nourished and grow well

in the environment created by devotion. Indeed, these graces grow nowhere else but here. The absence of a devotional spirit means death to the graces born in a renewed heart. True worship finds congeniality in the atmosphere made by a spirit of devotion. While prayer is helpful to devotion, at the same time devotion reacts on prayer, and helps us to pray.

Devotion engages the heart in prayer. It is not an easy task for the lips to try to pray while the heart is absent from it. The charge which God at one time made against his ancient Israel was, that they honored him with their lips while their hearts were far from him.

The very essence of prayer is the spirit of devotion. Without devotion prayer is an empty form, a vain round of words. Sad to say, much of this kind of prayer prevails, today, in the church. This is a busy age, bustling and active, and this bustling spirit has invaded the church of God. Its religious performances are many. The church works at religion with the order, precision and force of real machinery. But too often it works with the heartlessness of the machine. There is much of the treadmill movement in our ceaseless round and routine of religious doings. We pray without praying. We sing without singing with the Spirit and the understanding. We have music without the praise of God being in it, or near it. We go to church by habit, and come home all too gladly when the benediction is pronounced. We read our accustomed chapter in the Bible, and feel quite relieved when the task is done. We say our prayers by rote, as a schoolboy recites his lesson, and are not sorry when the Amen is uttered. (World Invisible, "Prayer and Devotion," https://1ref.us/1wl [accessed April 11, 2022])

It is through prayer and devotion that we structure our futures. If God is to be at the center of our new lives if we our indeed seeking true change, then we need to focus on Him. What we focus on day by day in our conscious minds is usually what ends up showing up in our lives at a later time in the future. You ever heard the phrase "Keep doing the same things the same way expecting a different result" (which is the definition of insanity, by the way)? We have the ability to control what we focus on. The morning time is usually the time when we are most in need of personal programming for setting the emotional tone for our entire day. If we are not using part of this time for prayer and devotion, then we are not programming our reticular activating systems with the things we want or need to focus on throughout the day to be highly productive. Consequently, the mind goes to the subconscious to find what to focus on. If you have a bad morning, then the mind searches in the negative filled areas of the subconscious mind because it matches the emotion. We set the tone by the stimuli we let dominate our mornings.

> As a man "thinketh in his heart, so is he." Many thoughts make up the unwritten history of a single day; and these thoughts have much to do with the formation of character. Our thoughts are to be strictly guarded; for one impure thought makes a deep impression on the soul. An evil thought leaves an evil impress on the mind. If the thoughts are pure and holy, the man is better for having cherished them. By them the spiritual pulse is quickened, and the power for doing good is increased. And as one drop of rain prepares the way for another in moistening the earth, so one good thought prepares the way for another. (White, *Messages to Young People*, p. 144)

Restructuring

Our environment has a huge role in the structuring of our behaviors. Anyone that says otherwise doesn't quite understand the laws of nature. In order to effectively provide a catalyst for change as well as provide a support system during the process of change ones' environment must be altered.

> For a good tree does not bear bad fruit, nor does a bad tree bear good fruit. For every tree is known by its own fruit. For *men* do not gather figs from thorns, nor do they gather grapes from a bramble bush. A good man out of the good treasure

of his heart brings forth good; and an evil man out of the evil treasure of his heart brings forth evil. For out of the abundance of the heart his mouth speaks. (Luke 6:43–45, NKJV)

A negative or evil environment can be like a tree, and its branches the people that make up this environment. The fruit is oftentimes the words and actions (behavior) that consistently come out of each person (branch) in this environment (tree). In the Bible it says that by beholding, we become changed (2 Cor. 3:18). If we are not firmly planted in God's Word, to learn what God's plan is for us, then we can be in danger of beholding the wrong spirit. All the spirits that retard our growth are the spirit of jealousy, envy, covetousness, lust, hatred, pride, gluttony, wrath, and sloth.

"But we all, with open face beholding as in a glass the glory of the Lord, are changed into the same image from glory to glory, even as by the Spirit of the Lord" (2 Cor. 3:18).

Being in these environments without the covering of the Lord will eventually lead to the total altering of one's behavior. So, if this has already happened and change is desired, it all starts first with restructuring one's personal environment, with the ultimate goal of change in the work, social, church, and other environmental behavior. As shown earlier in this book, our daily diets, exercises, prayer and devotion, conversations, music, jobs, etc., all play a vital role in how our behaviors are formed and remain. We have the control over the majority of the influencing factors in our lives. It just takes a choice, a choice to start today to change our daily routines.

Focus

Focus: the point of concentration. There are so many things in this world that are engineered simply to break FOCUS! By capturing it! When Abram was instructed by God to leave his land and to journey to another and to inhabit this Promised Land that was to endure to all his generations, he brought with him his brother's son, Lot. Along this journey they began to realize, because of the size of each of their camps, that they may need to separate. They both had a tremendous amount of livestock, which needed rich feeding grounds to survive. Abram gave Lot the first pick of which direction that he would go in and Abram would simply go in another direction and that would be that. Now, they both had a mission and knew the mission for it had been proclaimed by God. They both were focused on the mission. Well as I was saying, Lot made his decision:

> And Lot lifted up his eyes, and beheld all the plain of Jordan, that it was well watered every where, before the LORD destroyed Sodom and Gomorrah, even as the garden of the LORD, like the land of Egypt, as thou comest unto Zoar. Then Lot chose him all the plain of Jordan; and Lot journeyed east: and they separated themselves the one from the other. Abram dwelled in the land of Canaan, and Lot dwelled in the cities of the plain, and pitched his tent toward Sodom. But the men of Sodom were wicked and sinners before the LORD exceedingly. (Gen. 13:10–13)

As a result, he placed himself and his family in an environment that wasn't conducive to the mission at hand. I'm sure there weren't any problems at first but as time goes on, little by little, things began to change.

> And turning the cities of Sodom and Gomorrha into ashes condemned them with an overthrow, making them an ensample unto those that after should live ungodly; And delivered just Lot, vexed with the filthy conversation of the wicked: (For that righteous man dwelling among them, in seeing and hearing, vexed his righteous soul from day to day with their unlawful deeds;) the Lord knoweth how to deliver the godly out of temptations, and to reserve the unjust unto the day of judgment to be punished. (2 Peter 2:6–9)

Things began to happen to Lot and his family that deterred their focus from the mission at hand. Lot was captured and taken prisoner, his family became mesmerized by the way they lived in Sodom and Gomorrha so much so that it ended up costing his wife her life when they fled the city, because she didn't want to give it up. To top it all off, Lot ended up living in a cave in Zoar with his two daughters and they got him drunk and slept with him over the course of two nights and both became pregnant by him without him knowing (Gen. 14 and 19). Being in the wrong environment by choice often comes with a price. All of this was to make and keep Lot out of FOCUS.

Things happen in life all the time and that's what we all now call life, because we know there will always be distractions. But with God at the center of everything we do, He creates the level playing field at which we regain the focus needed to carry out His plan, but He must be consulted with daily. We are faced with snares daily, minute by minute, hour by hour, all with the intention to derail our momentum and to poison our souls, subsequently affecting our current outlooks, ultimately destroying our focus.

"And not only so, but we glory in tribulations also: knowing that tribulation worketh patience; And patience, experience; and experience, hope: And hope maketh not ashamed; because the love of God is shed abroad in our hearts by the Holy Ghost which is given unto us" (Rom. 5:3–5).

> We should **glory** (give very great praise and thanksgiving) in **tribulation** (grievous troubles, sufferings and afflictions) because we know that tribulation worketh **patience** (Quiet, steady perseverance, and makes us persistent in our course of action in spite of the difficulties) and patience gives us **experience** (a personal encounter, knowledge, practical wisdom that is gained from what we observe or have undergone) and experience, **hope** (gives us feelings that what we want can be had, or that the events that occurred will turn out for the best) hope, and this makes us not **ashamed** (distressed, timid or disgraced) because we now know that the love of God is shed abroad in our hearts by the Holy Ghost which is given unto us.
>
> —Faith Harris

Bibliography

"Antediluvian." Google. https://1ref.us/1vf (accessed March 25, 2022).

"Asterisk." Dictionary. https://1ref.us/1we (accessed April 11, 2022).

"Atlantis." Wikipedia. https://1ref.us/1w4 (accessed April 4, 2022).

Badgaiyan, Rajendra D. "Dopamine Is Released in the Striatum During Human Emotional Processing." National Library of Medicine. https://1ref.us/1wj (accessed April 11, 2022).

Bounds. E.M. "Chapter 3—Prayer and Devotion." World Invisible. https://1ref.us/1wl (accessed April 11, 2022).

"Breathing." Canadian Lung Association. https://1ref.us/1w1 (accessed April 1, 2022).

Cohut, Maria. "Serotonin Enhances Learning, Not Just Mood." Medical News Today. https://1ref.us/1vj (accessed March 30, 2022).

"Conception." Google. https://1ref.us/1vg (accessed March 28, 2022).

"Devote." Merriam-Webster. https://1ref.us/1wk (accessed April 11, 2022).

"Distraction." Google. https://1ref.us/1wx (accessed May 10, 2022).

"Dopamine." Wikipedia. https://1ref.us/1wr (accessed May 10, 2022).

Drye, Willie. "Atlantis." National Geographic. https://1ref.us/1w5 (accessed April 4, 2022).

"Dudley Allen Sargent." Wikipedia. https://1ref.us/1vs (accessed March 30, 2022).

Ettie, Gordon. "The Three Laws of Energy." The Book of Threes. https://1ref.us/1wb (accessed April 11, 2022).

"Gamma-aminobutyric Acid." Wikipedia. https://1ref.us/1wo (accessed May 10, 2022).

Gaskell, Adi. "Why We Think Multitasking Is More Efficient Than It Is." Forbes. https://1ref.us/1vc (accessed March 24, 2022).

"Getting Fresh Part 1: The Health Benefits of Fresh Air." Phantom Screens. https://1ref.us/1w2 (accessed April 1, 2022).

"Glutamine." Wikipedia. https://1ref.us/1wp (accessed May 10, 2022).

Gonzalez, Robbie. "What It Takes to Hold Your Breath for 24 Minutes (Yeah, It's a Thing)." Wired. https://1ref.us/1w0 (accessed April 1, 2022).

Gunnars, Kris. "How Much Water Should You Drink Per Day?" Healthline. https://1ref.us/1vw (accessed March 31, 2022).

"Health Benefits of L-Tyrosine." WebMD. https://1ref.us/1vm (accessed March 30, 2022).

"History of Physical Training and Fitness." Wikipedia. https://1ref.us/1vp (accessed March 30, 2022).

"History of Sport." Wikipedia. https://1ref.us/1vo (accessed March 30, 2022).

"Hypnosis." The Free Dictionary. https://1ref.us/1wg (accessed April 11, 2022).

"Image." Dictionary.com. https://1ref.us/1ve (accessed March 25, 2022).

"Industrial Revolution." Britannica. https://1ref.us/1vr (accessed March 30, 2022).

Kincaid, Danielle. "The Sherlock Holmes Conundrum, or The Difference Between Deductive and Inductive Reasoning." Medium. https://1ref.us/1wa (accessed April 4, 2022).

LeCorre, Erwan. "The History of Physical Fitness." MovNat. https://1ref.us/1vt (accessed March 30, 2022).

"Life definition." Google. https://1ref.us/1vd (accessed March 25, 2022).

"Likeness." Google. https://1ref.us/1wy (accessed May 10, 2022).

McCoy, Ryan. "FAQ—How Tall Were People Before the Flood?" Sealing Time Ministries. https://1ref.us/1w7 (accessed April 4, 2022).

Meilan, Solly. "A History of Gymnastics, From Ancient Greece to Tokyo 2020." Smithsonian Magazine. https://1ref.us/1vq (accessed March 30, 2022).

"Misdirection." Lexico. https://1ref.us/1wh (accessed April 11, 2022).

"Misdirection (magic)." Wikipedia. https://1ref.us/1wi (accessed April 11, 2022).

Montes, Cristina. "How Do Scientists Determine the Chemical Compositions of the Planets and Stars?" Astronomy. https://1ref.us/1wd (accessed April 11, 2022).

Nall, Rachel. "What Are the Benefits of Sunlight?" Healthline. https://1ref.us/1vx (accessed March 31, 2022).

"Neurotransmitter." Wikipedia. https://1ref.us/1vh (accessed March 29, 2022).

"Norepinephrine." Wikipedia. https://1ref.us/1wq (accessed May 10, 2022).

Petre, Alina. "7 Foods That Drain Your Energy." Healthline. https://1ref.us/1vk (accessed March 30, 2022).

"Prohibition." Britannica, https://1ref.us/1vz (accessed March 31, 2022).

"Protein in diet." MedlinePlus. https://1ref.us/1vl (accessed March 30, 2022).

"Quotes by Mark Matteson." BukRate. https://1ref.us/1w8 (accessed April 4, 2022).

Rosenberg, Matt. "Gregorian Calendar." ThoughtCo. https://1ref.us/1wc (accessed April 12, 2022).

Sahay, Amar, Kimberly N. Scobie, Alexis S. Hill, Colin M. O'Carroll, Mazen A. Kheirbek, Nesha S. Burghardt, André A. Fenton, Alex Dranovsky, and René Hen. "Increasing Adult Hippocampal Neurogenesis Is Sufficient to Improve Pattern Separation." Nature. https://1ref.us/1vn (accessed March 30, 2022).

Sharon, Nadav, Dr. "Antediluvian Knowledge." *The Torah*. https://1ref.us/1wu (accessed May 10, 2022).

"Solon." Wikipedia. https://1ref.us/1w6 (accessed April 4, 2022).

"Structure and Function of the Brain." Lumen. https://1ref.us/1wn (accessed May 10, 2022).

"Sunshine." Google. https://1ref.us/1vy (accessed March 31, 2022).

Swanson, Danielle, Robert Block, and Shaker Mousa. "Omega-3 Fatty Acids EPA and DHA: Health Benefits Throughout Life." https://1ref.us/1wt (accessed May 10, 2022).

"Symbolism (arts)." Wikipedia. https://1ref.us/1wf (accessed April 11, 2022).

"Trust." Lexico, https://1ref.us/1w3 (accessed April 1, 2022).

"Tyrosine." Wikipedia. https://1ref.us/1ws (accessed May 10, 2022).

Van De Walle, Gavin. "9 Important Functions of Protein in Your Body." Healthline. https://1ref.us/1vi (accessed March 29, 2022).

"Water." Wikipedia. https://1ref.us/1vv (accessed March 31, 2022).

"We Are What We Repeatedly Do." Daily Stoic. https://1ref.us/1w9 (accessed April 4, 2022).

White, Ellen G. *Christ's Object Lessons*. Washington, DC: Review and Herald, 1900.

———. *Counsels on Health*. Mountain View, CA: Pacific Press, 1923.

———. *Education*. Mountain View, CA: Pacific Press, 1903.

———. *Healthful Living*. Battle Creek, MI: Medical Missionary Board, 1897.

———. *In Heavenly Places*. Washington, D.C.: Review and Herald, 1967.

———. *Letters and Manuscripts*. Vol. 7. Ellen G. White Estate, 1891–1892.

———. *Letters and Manuscripts*. Vol. 11. Ellen G. White Estate, 1896.

———. *Letters and Manuscripts*. Vol. 13. Ellen G. White Estate, 1898.

———. *Lift Him Up*. Hagerstown, MD: Review and Herald, 1988.

———. *Messages to Young People*. Hagerstown, MD: Review and Herald, 1930.

———. *Mind, Character, and Personality*. Vol. 1. Nashville, TN: Southern Publishing Association, 1977.

———. *Our High Calling*. Washington, D.C.: Review and Herald, 1961.

———. *Patriarchs and Prophets*. Mountain View, CA: Pacific Press, 1890.

———. "Proper Education," *The Signs of the Times*, April 29, 1875

———. *Spiritual Gifts*. Vol. 4a. Battle Creek, MI: Seventh-day Adventist Publishing Association, 1864.

———. *Steps to Christ*. Mountain View, CA: Pacific Press, 1892.

———. *Testimonies for the Church*. Vol. 1. Mountain View, CA: Pacific Press, 1868.

———. *Testimonies for the Church*. Vol. 3. Mountain View, CA: Pacific Press, 1857.

———. *Testimonies for the Church*. Vol. 5. Mountain View, CA: Pacific Press, 1889.

———. *The Adventist Home*. Hagerstown, MD: Review and Herald, 1952.

———. *The Desire of Ages*. Mountain View, CA: Pacific Press, 1898.

———. *The Faith I Live By*. Washington, DC: Review and Herald, 1958.

TEACH Services, Inc.
P U B L I S H I N G

We invite you to view the complete
selection of titles we publish at:
www.TEACHServices.com

We encourage you to write us
with your thoughts about this,
or any other book we publish at:
info@TEACHServices.com

TEACH Services' titles may be purchased in
bulk quantities for educational, fund-raising,
business, or promotional use.
bulksales@TEACHServices.com

Finally, if you are interested in seeing
your own book in print, please contact us at:
publishing@TEACHServices.com

We are happy to review your manuscript at no charge.

www.ingramcontent.com/pod-product-compliance
Lightning Source LLC
Chambersburg PA
CBHW070543170426
43200CB00011B/2539